A NEW DAD'S GUIDE TO PLAYING GOD

A New Dad's Guide
To Playing God

Reflections on the Vocation of Fatherhood

JAMES PENRICE

ST PAULS

Alba
House

Library of Congress Cataloging-in-Publication Data

Penrice, James, 1961-
   A new dad's guide to playing God : reflections on the vocation of
fatherhood / James Penrice.
      p. cm.
Includes bibliographical references.
   ISBN 0-8189-0963-3
1. Fathers—Religious life. 2. Fatherhood—Religious
aspects—Christianity. I. Title.

BV4529.17.P46 2004
248.8'421—dc22

                                    2003022376

Produced and designed in the United States of America by the
Fathers and Brothers of the Society of St. Paul,
2187 Victory Boulevard, Staten Island, New York 10314-6603,
as part of their communications apostolate.

ISBN: 0-8189-0963-3

Printing Information:

Current Printing - first digit	1	2	3	4	5	6	7	8	9	10

Year of Current Printing - first year shown

2004	2005	2006	2007	2008	2009	2010	2011	2012

For my father,
William Penrice,
who showed me the way.

And for my wife Gina
and our children
Zachary, Elizabeth, and Nicholas
to whom I keep trying to play God.

Contents

A NEW DAD'S GUIDE TO PLAYING GOD

CHAPTER ONE

You Have the Right To Play God

Perhaps I should begin by explaining the title.

"Playing God" is not something we're normally encouraged to do. While it is socially acceptable to play devil's advocate, play the fool, play dumb, play hard to get, play your cards right, play the field, play dead or play to win, attempts to "play God" are usually met with some expression of, "How dare you!"

Strangely, the notion of "playing God" carries strictly negative connotations. The expression often refers to someone who sticks their nose where it doesn't belong, making decisions that impinge on others' freedom. "Playing God" often describes someone who is wrongly judgmental, who lords authority in a dictatorial fashion, or who decides to take vengeance through improper channels.

If we believe this is what it means to "play God," then is this truly what we believe about God? Does God stick his nose where it doesn't belong, or make decisions that impinge on people's freedom? Is God wrongly judgmental, lording his authority in a dictatorial fashion? Does God take vengeance through improper channels? Of course not. The negative connotations of "playing God" derive either from a misunderstanding of God, or the mistaken notion that human beings are not supposed to behave like God, or perhaps a little of both.

Yet when we really think about it, "playing God" — in the true sense of the term — is what *every human being* is called to do! Every one of us is created *in the image and likeness* of God. As such, we are all called to *act like him* — to be loving, forgiving, compassionate, to stand up for what's right, to actively pursue peace and justice. When we better understand God and our relationship with him, it becomes clear that our lives are to resemble the life of God as much as possible. We are to be his presence to everyone we meet — we are all called to "play God." We are reminded of this beautifully in these words of the Mass: "By the mingling of this water and wine *may we come to share in the divinity of Christ* who humbled himself to share in our humanity."

While the mandate to "play God" accompanies all human vocations, the call to parenthood requires it in a most exquisite way. Pope John Paul II wrote in his 1994 *Letter to Families*: "No living being on earth except man was created 'in the image and likeness of God.' Human fatherhood and motherhood, while remaining *biologically similar* to that of other living beings in nature, contain in an essential and unique way a 'likeness' to God which is the basis of the family as a community of human life, as a community of persons united in love."

When it comes to being an earthly father, this likeness takes on some very profound implications. When God calls us to be fathers he charges us with the mission to be the one from whom our children *will primarily experience the love of their heavenly*

Father. Jesus taught us to call God our Father, and it is through human fatherhood that we receive an intimate glimpse into this relationship. Fatherhood is really all about playing God! Our first responsibility as fathers is to discover that identity and do what it takes to nourish it.

Being a father means being the arms, eyes, heart and voice of God to our children. They will come to know God through their relationship with us — that's what we are all about. It is an awesome, humbling honor, yet an incredibly difficult and seemingly impossible task! When we deal with the myriad challenges of raising children, however, we gain a small glimpse into what it might be like to actually be God, for he faces even more challenges in trying to "raise" us!

We are continually growing into what God has created us to be, just as children grow through various stages of maturity. God continually lays out the expectations which we fail to meet. We certainly frustrate God as much as our kids frustrate us — even more so. God has to constantly balance his responsibility to discipline us with our need for tenderness and mercy. Sometimes it seems that my life would be much easier if I could completely control my children's behavior. Yet that would defeat the purpose of our family. Controlling my children's behavior would deny them the chance to grow into their own identity, to learn about life and its decisions and consequences. It would deny both my children and myself a true relationship with one another. God gave each of us a free will, and our poor decisions must be a constant source of frustration for him just as our children's misbehavior is for us. But it is the only way to grow in true love.

Children constantly ask "why." Many adults frequently ask

this same question of God. Sometimes we can answer those questions with an explanation. Sometimes we can't, if our child is not mature enough to understand the answer. So it is with many of our questions to God. There are answers to all of them, but often we are just not mature enough in our spiritual development to grasp them. We can either accept our limitations and trust that God has an answer even if we don't understand, or pout and rebel.

When my wife Gina and I were expecting our first child, the reaction from family and friends was completely positive. News of a first pregnancy is always met with excitement. When we shared news that our second child was conceived, some of the excitement was tempered by "warnings" of how much more work two kids can be over one. When Gina became pregnant with our third child, the news was met by many of our acquaintances with a reaction of, "Are you crazy?" In our culture the thought of parents being outnumbered by children seems unconventional, if not insane. In an age which prizes personal convenience and often views children as an obstacle to happiness, it is difficult for many to understand why a couple would want to have many children. After all of God's frustrations in trying to raise us, it must seem just as crazy for him to keep adding people to his family. But he does, because God is about life and love and community, not selfish interest and convenience. God keeps adding to his family despite the struggles and sacrifices involved, because he knows the overall result is worth the effort.

Just as God holds all power and strength over us, so do we over our children. They are small, weak and vulnerable. We have to always remember how much bigger we are and more powerful, and how easily that "advantage" can be abused. We are in charge, they are completely dependent upon us. We can't afford to let them down.

We have to sacrifice so much to give our children what they need. Children are incredibly demanding, they can exhaust us. We literally exhausted God to death through our disobedience. Unlike God, we don't always do everything right. That's when we need to trust that God will work through our weaknesses when we surrender our families to him and his paternal care.

While I know my own behavior is often not "God-like," reflecting on the similarities between God's parenthood and mine has increased my appreciation for God and his patience with me, and as such has increased my desire to be more God-like to my children by always calling upon him for help. Perhaps this is the real key to "playing God" to our children, constantly opening ourselves to God to allow him to use us as his instruments, realizing that by ourselves we can do nothing, but through us *he* can do everything.

The Scriptures are ripe with comparisons of human fatherhood to God's paternal care, and with reminders that we are indeed called to play God. I would like to share two of these as we begin our reflection. The book of Psalms tells us, "As a father has compassion on his children, so the Lord has compassion on the faithful" (Psalm 103:13). St. Paul writes, "Like a father with his own children, we exhorted you, encouraged you, and urged you to conduct yourselves in a manner worthy of God, who calls you to the glory of his Kingdom" (1 Thessalonians 2:11-12).

Pope John Paul II gave this outstanding definition of fatherhood in *Familiaris Consortio* (*The Role of the Christian Family in the Modern World*):

> In revealing and in reliving on earth the very father-
> hood of God, a man is called upon to ensure the har-
> monious and united development of all the members
> of the family: he will perform this task by exercising
> generous responsibility for the life conceived under
> the heart of the mother, by a more solicitous com-
> mitment to education, a task he shares with his wife,
> by work which is never a cause of division in the fam-
> ily but promotes its unity and stability, and by means
> of the witness he gives of an adult Christian life which
> effectively introduces the children into the living
> experience of Christ and the Church.

Revealing and reliving on earth the very fatherhood of God is a humbling and frightening mission. When I first learned that I was going to be a father, two conflicting emotions surged through me at once: great excitement and tremendous fear. The reality of becoming responsible for a new human life was fright-ening. Early on I began to fret over all of the obligations I was about to take on: spiritual, emotional, physical, financial. Like any other mere mortal I questioned my aptitude, and my doubts led to fears. After thirty-seven years of single life and just a few months into marriage, did I really have it in me to be a father?

When Gina and I went for the first ultrasound of our son Zachary, my fears were alleviated. As I watched the image on the monitor I was utterly amazed at what was being created in Gina's womb. We could see arms and hands, legs and feet, a strongly beating heart, a spine, eyes, and the halves of the brain. At one point Zachary's face turned towards us and his mouth opened as if in a yawn. Watching all this, something suddenly dawned on me which changed not only my outlook on my vocation to fatherhood, but on my calling as a Christian in general: This miraculous creative process was taking place, and Gina and I really had nothing to do with it. This new person was being created before our eyes, but not by us. Here I was so worried about how I would be able to care for a baby, but God was showing me through these images how much *he* was doing to care for it already! If God was working such a miracle for us, why did I need to worry? Gina and I simply gave the tiniest little pieces of ourselves, and with those infinitesimally small pieces, God was doing everything else! Viewing those ultrasound images made me truly realize what I had long known intellectually but needed to take to heart: God really is in charge! As much as I like to put life's demands and expectations on my own shoulders, God is really taking care of the things I can't do myself. That experience was also a reminder of the many other areas in my life for which I worry too much. If I can likewise give God just the tiniest little piece of myself, just think what he could do with it! Jesus alluded to this in the following parable, which carries a special message for parents:

> This is how the Kingdom of God is, like a man who throws seed upon the earth and sleeps and rises by night and day, and the seed sprouts and grows while he's unaware. The earth bears fruit on its own, first the shoot, then the head of grain, then the full grain in the head.... How may we compare the Kingdom

A NEW DAD'S GUIDE TO PLAYING GOD

of God, or in what parable can we present it? It's like a grain of mustard seed which, when it's sown upon the earth, is the smallest of all the seeds on the earth, yet when it's sown it grows and becomes the biggest of all the garden plants and puts out big branches, so that the birds of the sky are able to nest in its shade.

(Mark 4:26-28, 30-32)

As overwhelming as the responsibilities of parenthood can seem, God does not give us a mission without equipping us with everything we need to accomplish it. He never leaves us hanging out to dry. God chose to love a new little person into life, and he wanted someone to be his image to them, so *he chose us.* We were personally selected by God to be his image to the children he entrusted to our care. He does not set his loved ones up for failure. God will provide us whatever we need to accomplish any mission he gives us. St. Bernardine of Siena, in a sermon about St. Joseph (whom we will reflect upon in Chapter Three as the ideal role model for earthly fathers), put it this way: "There is a general rule concerning all special graces granted to any human being. Whenever the divine favor chooses someone to receive a special grace, or to accept a lofty vocation, God adorns the person chosen with all the gifts of the Spirit needed to fulfill the task at hand."

In his First Letter to the Corinthians, St. Paul said of love: "Love is patient, love is kind, it isn't jealous, doesn't boast, isn't arrogant. Love is not dishonorable, isn't selfish, isn't irritable, doesn't keep a record of past wrongs. Love doesn't rejoice at injustice, but rejoices in the truth. Love endures all things, love has complete faith and steadfast hope, love bears with every-

8

thing. Love never ends" (1 Corinthians 13:4-8). Note the order in which these attributes are listed. While all of the above are essential elements of love, it all begins with patience and kindness. Perhaps no human endeavor tests these qualities more intensely on a day to day basis than parenthood. Carefully and prayerfully re-read these words, meditating on their significance for your own fatherhood.

Just as in all Christian endeavors, while we strive to be the presence of God to others, we must see the presence of God in them as well. If we can recognize Jesus in "the least of his brothers and sisters," we will do a much more effective job of being his presence to them. Jesus consistently teaches how his presence is most strongly manifested in children:

> At that time the disciples came to Jesus and said, "Who's the greatest in the Kingdom of Heaven?" He called a child forward, stood it before them, and said, "Amen, I say to you, unless you turn about and become like children, you won't ever enter the Kingdom of Heaven! Therefore, whoever humbles himself like this child, he's the greatest in the Kingdom of Heaven. And whoever receives one such child in my name, receives me." (Matthew 18:1-5)

> See that you don't look down on one of these little ones, for I tell you, their angels in Heaven continually look upon the face of my Father in Heaven.... It isn't the will of your Father in Heaven that one of these little ones should be lost. (Matthew 18:10, 14)

> When the chief priests and the scribes saw the wonders he was performing and the children who were

shouting in the Temple and saying, "Hosanna to the Son of David!" they became indignant and said to him, "Do you hear what they're saying?" But Jesus replied, "Certainly. Haven't you read that 'out of the mouths of babes and nursing infants you have brought forth perfect praise'?"   (Matthew 21:15-16)

Then children were brought to him so he could lay his hands on them and pray, but the disciples rebuked him. Jesus said, "Let the children be, and don't stop them from coming to me, for of such as these is the Kingdom of Heaven!"   (Matthew 19:13-14)

Kathleen O. Chesto expresses the Christian parent's responsibility in this moving interpretation of the final judgment:

I have a vision. It is all of us standing before the Lord on judgment day. And the Lord will say, "I was hungry, and you fed me, thirsty, and you gave me a drink, naked and you clothed me, homeless and you sheltered me, imprisoned and you visited me...."
      (Matthew 25:36)
Puzzled, we'll respond:
      "When, Lord, when did I see you hungry?"
And the Lord will say:
      "How could you ask? You of the three and a half million peanut butter and jelly sandwiches, how could you even ask?"
      "But thirsty, Lord?"
      "I was in the Kool-Aid line that came in with the summer heat and the flies and left mud on your floor

and finger prints on your walls and you gave me a drink."

"Naked, Lord, homeless?"

"I was born to you naked and homeless and you sheltered me, first in wombs and then in arms and you clothed me with your love. And you spent the next twenty years keeping me in jeans."

"But imprisoned, Lord? I didn't visit you in prison. I was never in a prison."

"Oh yes, for I was imprisoned in my littleness, behind the bars of a crib and I cried out in the night and you came. I was imprisoned inside an eleven-year-old body that was bursting with so many new emotions I didn't know who I was and you loved me into being myself. And I was imprisoned behind my teenage rebellion, my anger, and my stereo set, and you waited outside my locked door for me to let you in.

"Now, beloved, enter into the joy which has been prepared for you from all eternity."

Before you continue reading any further, I want you to realize that I am by no means an expert on being a father. When a friend first suggested that I write a book about fatherhood, I did not take the idea very seriously. For one thing, I've only been a father for a few years, so I wasn't sure I had enough experience to offer any real insight. Secondly, I'm not so sure that even in these few years I've done that great a job. Two simple reflections helped me change my mind and get to work on the book you have begun to read.

As far as my minimal experience, I realized that while I'm

11

in no position to write a book on fatherhood in general, I do have something to offer to men becoming new fathers. As far as my inadequacy, I recalled some wonderful words of wisdom I was once given, which I would like to share with you.

I spent some time in a seminary, discerning a call to another kind of "fatherhood." One year I lived in a formation house with four other seminarians and two priests who were in charge of our formation. Our dinner conversations usually centered around sports, which classes we enjoyed complaining about, or other banal topics. One night at dinner, in an effort to steer us into some thoughtful conversation, one of the priests asked us, "What's your goal in life?" We rolled our eyes and thought, "Come on, Father, we're eating here." A few around the table offered some half-hearted answers to his question, then one of my house mates turned the tables on him. "What about you, Father?" he asked. "What's *your* goal in life?" The priest paused thoughtfully for a moment, then replied, "My goal in life... is to become a priest." We were obviously surprised by his response, and replied, "Well, great... congratulations! You made it!" He shook his head and said, "No, I haven't." Noting our puzzled expressions, he explained what he meant.

He told us that his ordination gave him the office and the faculties to perform the role of a priest. But *becoming* a priest — *becoming the kind of person who can most effectively live out that vocation* — is something he has to work towards every day of his life, and he is far from reaching that goal.

While I did not go on to become a priest, those wise words have stayed with me, and I apply them to my own vocation of marriage and fatherhood. Exchanging wedding vows with my wife did not make me a husband. Conceiving our children did not make me a father. I may have received those titles at those blessed moments and the promise of God's grace to fulfill them, but *becoming a husband and father* is something I have to continually work towards every day of my life, and I have quite a ways to go. So I offer you the reflections in this book not as an expert, but as a fellow learner (which is the literal meaning of the word "disciple") so that you may learn along with me about this beautiful vocation which God has entrusted to us.

What follows are various reflections on the vocation of fatherhood as understood in the Catholic Christian tradition. We will begin by reflecting on motherhood, for we cannot truly understand our identity as fathers unless we first realize the role of mothers, the bearers of all children. (In fact, the best way to love our children is to first love their mother.) Next we will reflect upon our ultimate role model as Christian fathers, St. Joseph, husband of Mary and earthly father of Jesus. We will also examine the lives of some other outstanding fathers from Scripture and the tradition of the Church. We will reflect on the sacrament of baptism and its importance to your child and to your family. I will encourage you to begin regular Mass attendance with your child beginning the week you bring them home — no matter how harrowing that experience may be. I will offer some reflections on the challenge of achieving balance among the many demanding aspects of our lives. We will address some special circumstances facing many fathers today: adoption, divorce, and death. We will conclude with some reflections on how fathers become heroes in some extraordinarily ordinary ways.

I realize that time is a precious commodity for new fathers. I will be honored to have you spend some of your time with this book, and it my ardent hope that in these pages you will find some inspiration to help you grow into the challenging yet infinitely rewarding vocation of playing God.

The "Weaker" Sex

I don't know who coined this curious expression to describe women, but I will venture two guesses: it must have been a man, and it must have been a man who never witnessed a woman giving birth. The three most incredible events I have personally witnessed a human being accomplish on this earth were my wife Gina giving birth to each of our three children. The strength, stamina and endurance it took to bring Zachary, Elizabeth and Nicholas forth from the womb was incredible; it was an ordeal I know I would never be able to undergo. There was nothing weak about the labor and delivery of our children. Watching Gina go through that reminded me of someone else who underwent a grueling physical ordeal some two thousand years ago, and I realized that she shared something in common with him that I would never have. Women are able to image the love of Jesus in a profound way which men simply can't. Perhaps no other human experience more closely resembles the Paschal Mystery of the passion, death and resurrection of Jesus Christ than labor and childbirth. The parallels are striking. Before we can begin to appreciate *our* role of being the image of the heavenly Father to our children, we need to understand how God's love is mirrored *first* through the instrument of their mother. This chapter is dedicated to appreciating a mother's role in God's plan.

Jesus endured his passion and death for one reason: to bring *us* life. He suffered not for his own gain, but for ours, so that we could be delivered from one kind of life into another, richer, more wonderful life than we could ever imagine or devise for ourselves. Jesus gave his own body and blood as the food which would sustain us to this new life. In eating his flesh and drinking his blood we indeed become one flesh and blood with him, united in an intimate familial bond.

Motherhood is a profound sign of this Paschal Mystery. When a woman gives birth she suffers not for her own sake, but for her child; she labors to bring her son or daughter from one kind of life into another, richer life. A mother gives her body and blood as food for her developing child to sustain them along this journey, and through this process the child indeed becomes one flesh and blood with her. A familial bond is established to help the child live this new kind of life, assured of all the love and support they will need.

Gestation, labor and childbirth is the Sacred Triduum — Holy Thursday, Good Friday and Easter — rolled into one blessed event. If this has never been made clear to you before, it is possibly due to a denigration of the vocation of motherhood which seems to have permeated our culture. Our society often views motherhood as an obstacle standing in the way of a woman's becoming fulfilled. Children are often seen as an inconvenience, instead of what they truly are: the fulfillment of marital love. In reality, for those who are called to it, motherhood *is* the fulfillment of womanhood. Likewise, for those who are called to it, fatherhood is the fulfillment of manhood. Like any other vocation from God, motherhood and fatherhood image him in such a way to make his love and glory more apparent to a skeptical world.

In his book *Tuesdays With Morrie*, sports writer Mitch Albom shares many enlightening conversations he had with Morrie Schwartz, his old college professor who was dying of ALS. The following excerpt offers encouragement to anyone struggling with the notion of children as an obstacle to a fulfilled life:

> Raising a family was one of those issues on my little list — things you want to get right before it's too late. I told Morrie about my generation's dilemma with having children, how we often saw them as tying us down, making us into these "parent" things that we did not want to be. I admitted to some of those emotions myself.... "Whenever people ask me about having children or not having children, I never tell them what to do," Morrie said now, looking at a photo of his eldest son. "I simply say, 'There is no experience like having children.' That's all. There is no substitute for it. You cannot do it with a friend. You cannot do it with a lover. If you want the experience of having complete responsibility for another human being, and to learn how to love and bond in the deepest way, then you should have children."

Scripture and tradition are rich in connections between the

Garden of Eden, where sin entered the world, and Calvary, where sin's ultimate consequence was vanquished. (Man's disobedience took place at a tree; his salvation is won on a tree. The Scriptures refer to Jesus as the new Adam; Catholic Church tradition upholds Mary as the new Eve.) Jesus' passion and death were necessary because human beings brought sin into the world (in Eden), and we needed the sacrifice of the Son of God (at Calvary) to make a true atonement for sin and to be reconciled with the Father. Because an understanding of what happened at the garden of Eden is essential to understanding what happened at Calvary — and because the creation story set in Eden is central to an understanding of masculinity and femininity — we will spend some time examining the parallels.

To begin, let's reflect upon the creation of man and woman as described in the second creation story in the Book of Genesis.

> The Lord God said: "It is not good for the man to be alone. I will make a suitable partner for him." So the Lord God formed out of the ground various wild animals and various birds of the air…. But none proved to be the suitable partner for the man. So the Lord God cast a deep sleep on the man, and while he was asleep, he took out one of his ribs and closed up its place with flesh. The Lord God then built up into a woman the rib that he had taken from the man. When he had brought her to the man, the man said: "This one, at last, is bone of my bones and flesh of my flesh; this one shall be called 'woman,' for out of 'her man' this one has been taken." That is why a man

leaves his father and mother and clings to his wife,
and the two of them become one body.
(Genesis 2:18-19a, 20b-24)

Sometimes this passage is misinterpreted as proclaiming
the superiority of men over women, especially in the context
of a marriage relationship. The famous television character
Archie Bunker once offered this passage as evidence to uphold
that view, saying that God created woman from a "spare rib —
a cheaper cut." Another Scripture passage which has also led to
the same misunderstanding is found in St. Paul's Letter to the
Ephesians: "Wives should be subject to their husbands as they
are to the Lord, for the husband is the wife's head just as Christ
is the head of the Church, and is himself the Savior of the body.
But just as the Church is subject to Christ, so too wives should
be subject to their husbands in everything." (Ephesians 5:22-
24)

Yet nothing could be further from the truth than the notion that God considers men superior to women, or that a husband is "in charge" of his wife. Examining these Scripture passages in the proper context will shed more light on the true relationship between men and women, and especially between
husbands and wives.

When the man saw the woman in the garden and said,
"This one, at last, is bone of my bone and flesh of my flesh," he
was expressing *her equality with him.* Up until this point God
had presented the man with many animals which were useful
as objects for food and clothing, but were not a suitable *partner*
for him. When God presented the woman, the man recognized
that now he truly had a *partner* — not merely another living

being to be used, but someone who is made of the same substance as he — someone who will share his human dignity. Thus from the very first pages of Scripture, men are reminded that women were given by God as *equal partners* in the stewardship of all of God's creation, and equal partners in their relationships.

When we read further into the above passage from Ephesians, we gain a broader understanding of what St. Paul is teaching us:

> Husbands, love your wives, just as Christ loved the Church and gave himself up for her, to sanctify her by cleansing her with the bath of water and the word. In this way he'll be able to present the Church to himself in its glory, having neither stain nor wrinkle nor anything of that sort, but instead holy and unblemished. In the same way husbands should love their wives just as they love their own bodies. The man who loves his wife loves himself, for no one ever hates his own flesh. On the contrary, he nourishes and cares for it just as Christ does for the Church. Because we're parts of his body.... Each one of you should in the same way love his wife as he loves himself, and the wife should respect her husband.
>
> (Ephesians 5:25-30, 33)

St. Paul tells husbands to "love your wives, just as Christ loved the Church." Exactly how did Christ love the Church? St. Paul tells us elsewhere in his Letter to the Philippians: "Have the same outlook among you that Christ Jesus had, who, though he was in the form of God, did not consider equality with God something to hold on to. Instead, he emptied himself and took on the form of a slave." (Philippians 2:5-7a)

Jesus' ultimate act of love was emptying himself — not grasping to his equality with God — and taking on the form of a *slave* in service to his Church. Jesus tells us often in the gospels that he came not to be served, but to serve, and to give his life for others. Jesus consistently showed his love by refusing places of honor. On the night before his crucifixion he washed the feet of the apostles — a task reserved only for servants — as an example to them of how they are to love. So how is a husband to love his wife as Christ loves the Church? *By serving her, and giving his life for her.* Husbands are not to lord themselves over their wives, but to empty themselves and give themselves in service.

So just what did St. Paul mean by wives being subject to their husbands in everything? We need to read three more verses from that passage to fill in the gaps. The introductory verse, addressed to both husbands and wives, dictates the need for *mutual* subjection: "Be subject *to one another* out of reverence for Christ" (Ephesians 5:21). Thus St. Paul's opening to this passage stresses that the same attitudes must be adopted by both spouses. St. Paul also adds the following significant insight into the sacramentality of marriage: "For this reason a man shall leave his father and mother and be joined to his wife, and the two shall become one flesh. This is a tremendous mystery. I'm applying it to Christ and the Church" (Ephesians 5:31-32). Throughout the Scriptures, marriage is used as a primary image to describe the covenant between God and his Church. (I will present a few more in Chapter Eight.) Here St. Paul is simply teaching what the Catholic Church has come to understand

and express in a profound way, that God created marriage as *an image of his covenant with his people*. In that covenant, the marriage of Jesus to the Church, *the Church is subject to Christ* who gave his life for her. But in the human reality of marriage, *both* partners are to love, honor and serve the other, and thus be subject to each other out of reverence for Christ, to whom we are truly subjects.

When speaking of marriage, Jesus says that a husband and wife are no longer two, but *one flesh*, with equal dignity and status before God. In *The Catechism of the Catholic Church* we read: "Since God created him man and woman, their mutual love becomes an image of the absolute and unfailing love with which God loves man.... The woman, 'flesh of his flesh,' i.e., his counterpart, his equal, his nearest in all things, is given to him by God as a 'helpmate'; she thus represents God from whom comes our help." (1604, 1605)

Pope John Paul II offers the following reflections on the equality of men and women, and the honored vocation of motherhood:

> Above all it is important to underline the equal dignity and responsibility of women with men. This equality is realized in a unique manner in that reciprocal self-giving by each one to the other and by both to the children which is proper to marriage and the family.... In creating the human race "male and female," God gives man and woman an equal personal dignity, empowering them with the inalienable rights and responsibilities proper to the human person. God then manifests the dignity of women in the highest

form possible, by assuming human flesh from the Virgin Mary, whom the Church honors as the Mother of God, calling her the new Eve and presenting her as the model of redeemed woman.... Authentic conjugal love presupposes and requires that a man have a profound respect for the equal dignity of his wife: "You are not her master," writes St. Ambrose, "but her husband; she was not given to you to be your slave, but your wife.... Reciprocate her attentiveness to you and be grateful to her for her love."

(Familiaris Consortio: The Role of the Christian Family in the Modern World)

Thank you, women who are mothers! You have sheltered human beings within yourselves in a unique experience of joy and travail. This experience makes you become God's own smile upon the newborn child, the one who guides your child's first steps, who helps it to grow and who is the anchor as the child makes its way along the journey of life.

(Letter to Women)

Human parenthood is something shared by both the man and the woman. Even if the woman, out of love for her husband, says: "I have given you a child," her words also mean: "This is our child." Although both of them together are parents of their child, *the woman's motherhood constitutes a special "part" in this shared parenthood,* and the most demanding part. Parenthood — even though it belongs to both — is

23

realized much more fully in the woman, especially in the prenatal period. It is the woman who "pays" directly for this shared generation, which literally absorbs the energies of her body and soul. It is therefore necessary that *the man* be fully aware that in their shared parenthood he owes *a special debt to the woman*.... The man — even with all his sharing in parenthood — always remains "outside" the process of pregnancy and the baby's birth; in many ways he has to *learn* his own *"fatherhood" from the mother*.... Motherhood has been introduced into the order of the Covenant that God made with humanity in Jesus Christ. Each and every time that *motherhood* is repeated in human history, it is always *related to the Covenant* which God established with the human race through the motherhood of the Mother of God.

(*Mulieris Dignitatem*)

Returning to the Garden of Eden, we know where the story goes from where we left off. The serpent, signifying the devil, slithers into the garden and tempts the woman to eat of the tree of which God had forbidden the man and the woman to eat. She succumbs to the temptation, then persuades the man to eat of the tree as well. When God confronts them with their offense, they both point the finger of blame elsewhere — the man blames the woman, the woman blames the serpent. God reminds them that there is plenty of blame to go around, and each will face a consequence for their disobedience. God's words to the serpent and to the woman hold special significance:

The "Weaker" Sex

To the serpent he said, "I will put enmity between
you and the woman, and between your offspring and
hers; he will strike at your head, while you strike at
his heel." To the woman he said, "I will intensify the
pangs of your childbearing; in pain shall you bring
forth children."…The man called his wife Eve, because she became the mother of all the living.

(Genesis 3:15-16a, 20)

Already in this passage, there is the promise of salvation
for humanity, and that salvation is promised *through a woman.*
We've already discussed the way that labor pains can be a sign
of God's redemptive love, imaging the suffering of Christ. Yet
the promise of salvation is most eloquently stated in God's words
to the serpent. The serpent represents the devil and his evil
forces. By saying "I will put enmity between you and the woman,
and between your offspring and hers; he will strike at your head
while you strike at his heel," God is saying that there will always be tension between the forces of evil and good. But he is
also promising that good will always have the upper hand, and
eventually the victory. While evil can only strike at humanity's
heel, thus causing pain and trouble, humanity can strike at evil's
head, and thus ultimately conquer it. Thus even from the dawn
of sin, God is promising his people that they will be saved from
the ultimate consequence of sin.

It is significant that the woman was the first to be tempted
and to fall into sin; for God ordered humanity so that *everything*
— including our salvation — would begin through women. Since
sin entered the world *through a woman,* salvation would enter

25

the world *through a woman* as well — Jesus coming to us through Mary. While *the first man*, responded to sin by following suit, sin would be vanquished by a *man* who would refuse to give into temptation and who would choose to give his life so that people could conquer sin. This is why Scripture later refers to Jesus as the new Adam, and Church tradition upholds Mary as the new Eve:

> Adam, the first man, became a living being; the last Adam became a life-giving spirit. But the spiritual isn't first; first comes the physical, then comes the spiritual. The first man was made of dust, the second man came from Heaven. Those who are of the dust are like the man of dust, and those who are of Heaven are like the man from Heaven, and just as we've borne the image of the man of dust, so too we'll bear the image of the man from Heaven.
>
> (1 Corinthians 15:45-49)

> Just as one man's offense resulted in condemnation for all, so too one man's obedience results in pardon and life for all. For just as many were made sinners as a result of one man's disobedience, so too through one man's obedience many will be made righteous.
>
> (Romans 5:18-19)

> The Father of mercies willed that the incarnation should be preceded by the acceptance of her who was predestined to be the mother of His Son, so that just as a woman contributed to death, so also a woman

should contribute to life. Hence not a few of the early Fathers gladly assert in their preaching, "The knot of Eve's disobedience was untied by Mary's obedience; what the virgin Eve bound through her unbelief, the Virgin Mary loosened by her faith." Comparing Mary with Eve, they call her "the Mother of the living," and still more often they say: "death through Eve, life through Mary." *(Lumen Gentium,* 56)

The Virgin Mary "cooperated through free faith and obedience in human salvation." She uttered her yes "in the name of all human nature." By her obedience she became the New Eve, mother of the living.

(Catechism, 511)

God's plan for humanity still relies on the cooperation of women, just as it did at the time of his coming to earth incarnate. This is why Mary is such an important figure, and a reminder of the sacred place of all women, particularly mothers, in God's plan of salvation.

Traditional Catholic art has long recognized this in popular depictions of Mary. Often in statues and paintings Mary is shown stepping on the head of a serpent. With the coming of Mary, humanity is now striking at the head of evil, preparing to deal its death blow. This proclaims the truth that Mary ushered in the age of salvation, because it was through her fiat — her "yes" to God — that Jesus the savior would come into the world.

Earlier in this chapter I wrote that in our culture children are often seen as an obstacle to the fulfillment of womanhood, instead of its actual fulfillment. The proliferation of the contraception and abortion industries attest to this. No chapter on the dignity of motherhood would be complete without reference to these disturbing trends in our culture. I would like to share some insights on these matters from some great Catholic leaders of our time.

Speaking of a "contraceptive mentality," Pope John Paul II writes in *Evangelium Vitae* (*The Gospel of Life*): "The life which could result from a sexual encounter… becomes an enemy to be avoided at all costs, and abortion becomes the only decisive response to failed contraception."

Commenting on Pope Paul VI's 1968 encyclical *Humanae Vitae* (*Of Human Life*) Archbishop Charles Chaput writes:

> Contraception might be marketed as liberating for women, but the real "beneficiaries" of birth control would be men. Three decades later, exactly as Pope Paul VI warned, contraception has largely released males from responsibility for their sexual behavior. Ironically, while many feminists have attacked the Catholic Church for her alleged disregard of women, the Church in *Humanae Vitae* rejected sexual exploitation of women *years before that message entered the cultural mainstream.…* Predictably, in the name of the "freedom" provided by contraception and abortion, an exaggerated feminism has undermined the humanity of women. A man and a woman take part uniquely in the glory of God by their ability to create new life with Him. At the heart of contraception, however, is the idea that fertility is an infection that must be attacked, exactly as antibiotics attack bacteria. Here

we can also easily spot the link between contraception and abortion. If fertility can be misrepresented as an infection to be attacked, *so, too, can new life.* In either case, a key element of woman's identity — her potential for bearing new life — is recast as a weakness requiring distrust and "treatment." Woman becomes the object of the tools she relies upon to ensure her own liberation. Man takes no share of the burden.

The pure, human act of intercourse holds no boundaries, just as there are no boundaries to the love between husband and wife of which intercourse is the fullest expression. In a pure, natural act of sexual union, the fullest expression of love, the couple gives *everything* to each other — holding nothing back. Artificial birth control prevents this total giving, making it a limited and conditional sharing between the partners. Any relationship based on conditions and limits rather than total sharing is less than pure human love, and is opening itself up to the problems that naturally occur when pure unconditional love is not central to a relationship. If a couple withholds complete sexual union from each other, they can withhold other things as well. This withholding leads to other problems which can eventually lead to the breakup of the relationship. In the United States there is widespread use of artificial birth control. There is also about a 50% divorce rate. It is difficult to deny a connection between the withholding of physical love and the withholding of spiritual and emotional love.

In our earlier readings from St. Paul, we saw that Jesus emptied himself and took the form of a slave. In the act of sexual union — designed as a sign of God's total giving to his Church — the husband empties himself into his wife. The implications of this act go far beyond the bedroom. We cannot empty ourselves into our wives in the sexual union and not do so in the rest of our life. Anything we withhold in one area, we will withhold in another. Our wives deserve nothing less than all of us, all the time, for that is what Christ has given the Church. We need to give ourselves to them on a daily basis.

Far from being the "weaker sex," women bear the strength which brings and nurtures children into the world, and thus have a primordial role in God's plan for humanity. We need to honor and respect them if we are to truly fulfill our role as fathers.

When one finds a worthy wife, her value is far beyond pearls. Her husband, entrusting his heart to her, has an unfailing prize. She brings him good, and not evil, all the days of her life.... She is girt about with strength, and sturdy are her arms. She enjoys the success of her dealings; at night her lamp is undimmed. She puts her hands to the distaff, and her fingers ply the spindle. She reaches out her hands to the poor, and extends her arms to the needy. She fears not the snow for her household; all her charges are doubly clothed. She makes her own coverlets; fine linen and purple are her clothing. Her husband is prominent at the city gates as he sits with the elders of the land. She makes garments and sells them, and stocks the merchants with belts. She is clothed with strength and dignity, and she laughs at the days to come. She opens her mouth in wisdom, and on her tongue is kindly counsel. She watches the conduct of her household, and eats not her food in idleness. Her children rise up and praise her; her husband, too, extols her: "Many are the women of proven worth, but you have excelled them all." Charm is deceptive and beauty fleeting; the woman who fears the Lord is to be praised. Give her a reward of her labors, and let her works praise her at the city gates.

(Proverbs 31:10-13, 17-31)

Chapter Three

Be a Regular Joe

We have no greater role model in our vocation as Christian husbands and fathers than St. Joseph, husband of Mary and earthly father of Jesus. In Chapter One I quoted St. Bernardine of Siena from a sermon he gave on St. Joseph, speaking of the gifts God grants to everyone he calls to a lofty vocation. St. Bernardine's sermon continues:

> This general rule is especially verified in the case of Saint Joseph, the foster-father of our Lord and the husband of the Queen of our world, enthroned above the angels. He was chosen by the eternal Father as the trustworthy guardian and protector of his greatest treasures, namely, his divine Son and Mary, Joseph's wife. He carried out this vocation with complete fidelity until at last God called him, saying: "Good and faithful servant, enter into the joy of your Lord."

We were chosen by the eternal Father as the trustworthy guardian and protector of more of his greatest treasures: our wives and children. When we carry out this vocation with complete fidelity God will likewise call us, as good and faithful servants, into the joy of the Lord.

The gospels don't tell us very much about St. Joseph. But the glimpses they offer give us a wealth of reflection on this holy man. We will examine what the gospels do have to tell us about St. Joseph to gain more insight into his relationship with Jesus and with us, and to learn how he can be our guide in raising our children.

We will begin with the introduction of Mary in the Gospel of Luke. Though Joseph is mentioned only briefly in this passage, an exploration of these verses will shed much light on his role as husband and father:

> In the sixth month the angel Gabriel was sent from God to a city of Galilee named Nazareth, to a virgin who was betrothed to a man of the house of David named Joseph, and the virgin's name was Mary. And when he came into her presence he said, "Hail, full of grace, the Lord is with you!" She was perplexed by these words and wondered what sort of greeting this could be. Then the angel said to her, "Fear not, Mary — you have found grace before the Lord. And, behold, you will conceive in your womb and will bear a son, and you shall name him Jesus. He will be great and will be called Son of the Most High, and the Lord God will give him the throne of his father, David. He will reign over the house of Jacob forever, and his Kingdom will have no end." Mary said to the angel, "How will this come about, since I do not know man?"
> (Luke 1:26-34)

Reading this passage in English, from a twenty-first century American perspective, Mary's response to the angel makes little sense: "How will this come about, since I do not know man?" (referring to having sexual relations with a man). If the angel had told Mary that she had already conceived a child, her question would be understandable: "How can I, a virgin, have conceived a child?" But note that the angel did *not* tell Mary that she *had already conceived*, but that she *will* conceive. It hasn't happened yet; it is going to. The fact that she is a virgin up to this point in her life is irrelevant to the angel's message.

Furthermore, we were told a few verses earlier that at the time of the angel's visit Mary was betrothed to Joseph. Now for an angel — or anyone else, for that matter — to tell a young woman preparing for marriage that she will conceive a child would seem to us a perfectly reasonable expectation. Yet it was not for Mary, for the expressed reason which our modern English translations render, "How will this come about, since I do not know man?" Why was Mary so puzzled about the news of this conception? To discover the answer, we first need to understand something about the language in which this gospel was written, and about the culture in which Mary and Joseph lived.

Luke wrote his gospel in Greek, and in the original text the verb in "I do not know man" was written in the present absolute tense. This means that Mary was referring to virginity not only in the past and present, but in the future as well. In explaining this point, Scripture scholar Rene Laurentin offers the following example: "If someone to whom a cigarette is offered replies, 'I don't smoke,' he is understood to mean, 'I never smoke,' and not 'I am not smoking right now.'" When Mary said she does not know man, she meant that this is a *permanent con-*

dition. Mary never intended to have sexual relations, even in marriage. At the time of their betrothal, Mary and Joseph had committed themselves to perpetual virginity.

Why would they have done this? In our society, where sex outside of marriage is so common, the thought of a married couple purposely abstaining from intercourse strikes us as odd. Furthermore, in our modern Catholic theology of marriage, consummation is an expectation, as is the openness to procreation. Yet in Mary and Joseph's day it was not at all uncommon for married couples to consecrate themselves to virginity for religious reasons. We have ample evidence from Scripture — in this passage and several others — to conclude that Mary and Joseph entered into this kind of consecration.

This tells us a great deal about Joseph. First, he was a devoutly religious man, willing to sacrifice both the pleasure of sexual intercourse and any prospect of having children, in order to serve God in the way he was called. He was motivated to marriage not by passion or lust, but by a thoughtful and prayerful dedication to God and to Mary. His sacrifice meant not only a lot to Mary, it means a great deal to us today. Mary's perpetual virginity is an important Christological truth, since *everything* we hold about Mary is directly related to what we believe about Jesus. Without Mary's perpetual virginity — and Joseph's willingness to allow this to happen — everything we believe about Jesus becomes watered down. Allow me to explain.

Through her Immaculate Conception, Mary was preserved from the stain of original sin so that she would be a pure and holy vessel in which to conceive and nurture the Son of God. (For the sinless Son of God could not be conceived in someone with original sin, for he would thus inherit it as well.) It would thus be completely inappropriate, given Mary's unique place in salvation history, for her womb to conceive and bear other children. There was something unique about the body and blood which was to be conceived and nourished in Mary's womb — it was the sinless body and blood which would one day be sacrificed for the salvation of the world, and given to us as the food and drink which would give us true life. As great a man as Joseph was, he was still conceived with original sin, and any child he would have conceived with Mary would bear this stain as well. The idea that Jesus — whose body and blood would be sacrificed for the salvation of the world — would have brothers or sisters tainted by original sin sharing his body and blood lines would denigrate the unique and sacred character of the Eucharist. Mary's womb was one of a kind, meant for only one *very special* child, the Son of God. The idea of that same womb conceiving and bearing any other child just doesn't add up.

The following example may help put things into perspective. I work at a Catholic Church as the Director of Religious Education. Suppose I came to work one morning with a turkey sandwich for my lunch. When I arrived for work, I would look for a place to store my sandwich until lunch time. So let's say I decide to put it in the tabernacle along with the Blessed Sacrament. Would this really be an appropriate place to store my lunch? Certainly not. Not that there is anything inherently wrong with that turkey sandwich; in itself it is a very good thing. It is a healthy food which will give me nourishment to get me through my day. But when we think of why that tabernacle was made and what is housed inside, we realize that the turkey sandwich — as good as it is — just doesn't belong there.

So it is with the notion of Joseph having relations with Mary and the two conceiving other children. In the grand picture of our salvation, it is not appropriate. Thus the sacrifice to which Joseph committed himself before his betrothal to Mary provided tremendous dividends to generations after him, though he did not realize it at the time.

In a similar way, the sacrifices we are called to make in our family life will pay dividends for generations after us which we may never realize. It is a part of the trust we put in God when we commit ourselves to marriage. When a couple gets married, they really have no idea what they are getting into. They know they are doing something important for God and for each other, but only as the years go by do they begin to see the implications. Some of the greatest fruit of their sacrifices they may never see, for they may only be fulfilled in generations long past their lifetime. No one knows on their wedding day what joys and tragedies await them in their lives together. A couple approaches the altar with really only three things: faith, hope and love. With these three gifts God can accomplish great things if we are willing to persevere. (I will reflect on this point a little further in Chapter Five.)

The most detailed accounts we have of Joseph are in the Gospel of Matthew. Let's read what this gospel has to tell us. In Matthew's first chapter we read the following:

> Now the birth of Jesus Christ came about in the following manner. When his mother Mary was betrothed to Joseph, but before they came together, she was found to be with child by the Holy Spirit. Joseph her husband was a good and upright man so he was

planning to put her away, but quietly because he didn't wish to disgrace her. But while he was thinking these things over, behold, an angel of the Lord appeared to him in a dream and said, "Joseph son of David, don't be afraid to take your wife Mary into your house — the child who has been conceived in her is from the Holy Spirit. She'll give birth to a son and you shall name him Jesus, because he'll save his people from their sins." All this took place to fulfill what was declared by the Lord through the prophet when he said, "Behold, the virgin shall be with child and will give birth to a son, and they shall give him the name Emmanuel, which is translated, 'God with us.'" When Joseph rose from his sleep he did as the angel of the Lord had commanded him and took his wife into his house.   (Matthew 1:18-24)

In Mary and Joseph's day a betrothal was the entrance into a marriage agreement, but the marriage was not fulfilled until the woman entered the man's home to live with him. This is what is meant by, "When his mother Mary was betrothed to Joseph, but before they came together...." Now put yourself in Joseph's shoes. You have agreed to marry a sweet young woman. But she is soon found to be pregnant, and you had nothing to do with it. The hurt and the anger Joseph experienced must have been great. According to the law of the time, a woman in Mary's situation was to be stoned to death. Joseph knew this; all he had to do was notify the authorities, and Mary would have received this punishment. But in the midst of his hurt Joseph was not seeking vengeance or retribution; he did not adopt a "Let her

A NEW DAD'S GUIDE TO PLAYING GOD

get what's coming to her" attitude. What mattered most to Joseph was what was best for Mary. He was not going to stay with her if she proved to be unfaithful, but he did not want her harmed, either. This is what is meant by, "He was planning to put her away, but quietly because he didn't wish to disgrace her."

Yet when an angel appeared in a dream to let him know what really happened, Joseph was obedient to the Lord, taking Mary as his wife and Jesus as his son. Through this incident Joseph displayed some powerful traits which are indispensable for being a good husband and father. He was a just man, caring for the well-being of someone he had committed to love, putting her needs before his own feelings. He was forgiving, able to let go of a grudge, and to resist the pull of what popular culture was telling him to do. (As in Joseph's day, forgiveness towards someone who has hurt us badly also goes against the grain of our popular culture. Have you ever noticed that when someone is able to forgive terrible wrongs, such as people forgiving someone who murdered a family member, it makes news headlines? In the Christian life, such forgiveness is supposed to be commonplace.) And even when his human reason failed to make sense of the situation, Joseph believed in the revelation of God and trusted that everything would be all right. Hoping in God's promise, Joseph put aside his fears and human rationality and did what God asked him to do. Generations since have reaped the rewards of his decisions and sacrifices, as will the generations who follow us in our own family trees.

God was also asking Joseph to radically change the plans he had made for his life. Joseph and Mary did not anticipate having children — they were planning on a quiet little home in Nazareth without the pitter-patter of little feet. Now not only was there a child in the picture, but God's own Son, conceived by the Holy Spirit, destined to save humanity from its sins. What an incredible responsibility to which Joseph assented, even though it meant sacrificing his own convenience and abandoning his own plans and ambitions.

Nothing turns our life's routines and plans more upside down than the birth of a child. It is incredible how one little person can so disrupt *everything* in our lives! Suddenly we can no longer do whatever we want to do; our lives are now centered on this little person and their needs, and the unique needs our wives suddenly have now that they are mothers as well. Like Joseph, we must sacrifice our own convenience and abandon plans and ambitions we may have had before our children came. Our lives are now very different, and harried though they are, the much richer they have become.

Let's read what else the Gospel of Matthew has to tell us about Joseph. We pick up the story after Jesus' birth and the visit of the Magi.

> When they had departed, behold, the angel of the Lord appeared in a dream to Joseph and said, "Get up, take the child and its mother and flee to Egypt and stay there until I tell you — Herod is going to search for the child to kill it." So Joseph got up and took the child and its mother and departed by night for Egypt, and he stayed there until Herod's death to fulfill what was stated by the Lord through the prophet when he said, "I called my son out of Egypt."
> (Matthew 2:13-15)

After Herod died, an angel of the Lord appeared in a dream to Joseph in Egypt and said, "Get up, take the child and its mother and go to the land of Israel — those who sought the child's life are dead." So Joseph got up and took the child and its mother and went into the land of Israel. But when he heard that Archelaus was ruling over Judea in place of his father Herod he was afraid to go there; so, having been warned in a dream, he departed for the district of Galilee, and he went and settled in a town called Nazareth to fulfill what was written by the prophets, "He shall be called a Nazorean."

(Matthew 2:19-23)

There are some consistent traits in both of these passages. First, most of what Matthew tells us about Joseph happens while he is asleep. Joseph is visited by angels at key moments who give him God's next set of instructions for his family. Perhaps as a hard working carpenter and father of a newborn baby, Joseph is so busy that his sleeping hours are the only times God can get his attention! In any event, Joseph experiences something all new fathers can relate to: having his sleep interrupted quite often with messages about his child's needs. With us it's our children themselves giving us nocturnal revelations that they are hungry, or gaseous, or lonely, or simply cannot sleep. An image that may help get you through those long, frustrating nights — when you're wondering if you're *ever* going to get another good night's sleep — is that of Joseph receiving his angelic instructions. Your night time visits with your child are no less sacred. You are also receiving a message from God through this precious instrument he has entrusted to your care. During those wee hours of the night you are holding your little angel. Recognize that, listen, and respond.

Another consistent element in these passages is that Joseph is instructed to do something for his family in order to fulfill what the prophets had written, to bring about God's plan of salvation for his Church. Your family also plays a crucial role in God's saving plan, for you are the foundational unit of the Church. The documents of the Second Vatican Council repeatedly refer to the family as "the domestic church." Pope John Paul II has stated, "The family itself is the first and most appropriate place for teaching the truths of the faith, the practice of Christian virtues and the essential values of family life." Pope Leo XIII wrote that "the family was ordained of God.... It was before the Church, or rather the first form of the Church on earth." Pope Paul VI declared, "There should be found in every family the various aspects of the entire Church." The U.S. Bishops wrote in their pastoral plan *Our Hearts Were Burning Within Us*: "There may be no place more significant for catechesis than the family." Kathy Coffey writes, "Our first, most precious learning about God can only come at home. If, in that small sphere, we do not fall in love with God, it would be pointless to continue our quest."

Like Joseph, you are also to listen to God's messages to fulfill his plan for your domestic church, and as such help to bring about their salvation and to build up the broader Body of Christ.

In all of these episodes, Joseph is called upon to take on personal inconvenience and hardship in order to protect his family. There was a lot of traveling involved in the passages we just read. In those days traveling was not as convenient as it is today. There were no airlines or automobiles, everything had to be traversed by foot or on the back of an animal. The course of Joseph's travels as described in these passages covered several hundred miles, in heat and wilderness conditions. Doing this kind of travel with a newborn infant was even more challenging. Joseph was called upon to spend himself for the good of his family. We as fathers are called to do the same in many different ways.

We know that Joseph was poor, as evidenced by the sacrifice he and Mary offered at the presentation of the baby Jesus in the Temple: "When the day came for their purification according to the Torah of Moses they took the child up to Jerusalem to present him to the Lord — as it is written in the Torah of the Lord, 'every firstborn male shall be called holy to the Lord' — and to offer a sacrifice according to what is said in the Torah of the Lord, 'a pair of turtle doves or two young pigeons'" (Luke 2:22-24). The sacrifice of turtle doves or pigeons was to be offered by those who could not afford the more expensive sacrifice of a lamb called for in the Torah. Joseph certainly must have been beset by financial worries as he prepared to take on the responsibility of a family, even with the knowledge that he was raising the Son of God, and the certainty that God would provide for him. As Christian fathers we realize that our children are a miracle from God, that our children are really his, and that he will provide for them. But we still worry about what we have to do to make ends meet. In addition to the reflection I presented in Chapter One about seeing the ultrasound images of my first child, I give you the following words of Jesus to comfort you in such times of worry:

Do not worry about your life, what you'll eat, or
about your body, what you'll wear; isn't life more
than food, and the body more than clothing? Look
at the birds of the sky — they neither sow nor reap
nor gather into barns, yet your Heavenly Father feeds
them; aren't you worth more than they are? But
which of you can add any time to your life by worrying? And why do you worry about clothing? Look at
how the lilies of the field grow; they neither work nor
spin. But I tell you, even Solomon in all his glory
wasn't arrayed like one of them. But if God so clothes
the grass of the fields, which is here today and thrown
into the oven tomorrow, won't he clothe you much
better, O you of little faith? So don't go worrying,
saying, "What will we eat?" or, "What will we drink?"
or, "What will we put on?" for the Gentiles seek all
those things. Your Heavenly Father knows you need
them! But first seek the Kingdom and the will of God
and all those things will be given to you also.

(Matthew 6:25-33)

The final mention of Joseph in the gospels comes in the
passage I am about to share from the Gospel of Luke. When
Jesus was twelve years old he remained in Jerusalem after the
feast of Passover while Joseph and Mary traveled home. When
they realized Jesus was not with them, Joseph and Mary returned to Jerusalem and spent three days searching for him.
Imagine searching for your child for three days in a large,
crowded city, and the anguish this must have brought Joseph
and Mary. Finally, they find him:

And it happened that after three days they found him in the Temple, seated in the midst of the teachers, both listening to them and asking them questions, and all those listening to him were amazed at his intelligence and his answers. When his parents saw him they were amazed, and his mother said to him, "Son, why did you do this to us? You see your father and I have been looking for you, worried to death!" And he said to them, "Didn't you know that I have to concern myself with my Father's affairs?" And they didn't understand what he was telling them. (Luke 2:46-50)

Mary names Joseph as Jesus' father, saying, "Your father and I have been looking for you." In Jesus' response, he calls God his Father, saying, "Didn't you know that I have to concern myself with my Father's affairs?" This is a reminder to us that while we are given the title "father," and all the responsibilities that go with it, God is really the Father of our children. We hold them for a time; God holds them forever. We are stewards of our children, and one day God will take them back to himself. We need to keep that ever in mind to put our fatherhood into its true perspective.

I would like to conclude this chapter by sharing with you the intercessions and closing prayer from Evening Prayer II (from the Liturgy of the Hours) for the Feast of St. Joseph on March 19, for they sum up much of what we have been reflecting upon:

All fatherhood in heaven and on earth has its origin in God. Let us turn to him and pray:

Our Father in heaven, hear our prayer.

All-holy Father, you revealed to St. Joseph your eternal plan of salvation in Christ,

— deepen our understanding of your Son, true God and true man.

Father in heaven, you feed the birds of the air, and clothe the fields with the fruit of the earth,

— give all your children their daily bread, to sustain soul and body.

Maker of the universe, you have entrusted your creation to our safekeeping,

— may all who work receive a just reward for their labors.

God of all righteousness, you want us all to be like you,

— may St. Joseph inspire us to walk always in your way of holiness.

Look kindly on the dying and the dead, and grant them your mercy,

— through the intercession of Jesus, Mary and Joseph.

Father, you entrusted our Savior to the care of St. Joseph. By the help of his prayers may your Church continue to serve its Lord, Jesus Christ, who lives and reigns with you and the Holy Spirit, one God, for ever and ever. Amen.

CHAPTER FOUR

The Dad's Club

While St. Joseph is the ultimate example of a Christian Father, the Scriptures and the tradition of the Church give us other outstanding role models as well. Let's consider a few of them.

Abraham

Abraham is called the "Father of the Faith," for it was with Abraham that God established the original covenant with the people of Israel from which Christianity sprung. Abraham was promised many descendants as a sign of the covenant. He found it hard to believe that he would have children, as he and his wife Sarah were quite elderly. But God blessed them with a child as a sign of his faithfulness. Our children are no less a sign of God's faithfulness, and an example to the world of his infinite love.

The child born to Abraham and Sarah was named Isaac. When the boy grew older, God put Abraham's faith to a rather dramatic test, as shown in the following story:

God put Abraham to the test. He called to him, "Abraham!" "Ready!" he replied. Then God said: "Take your son Isaac, your only one, whom you love, and go to the land of Moriah. There you shall offer him up as a holocaust on a height that I will point out to you." Early the next morning Abraham saddled his donkey, took with him his son, Isaac, and two of his servants as well, and with the wood that he had cut for the holocaust, set out for the place for which God had told him.

On the third day Abraham got sight of the place from afar. Then he said to his servants: "Both of you stay here with the donkey, while the boy and I go over yonder. We will worship and then come back to you." Thereupon Abraham took the wood for the holocaust and laid it on his son Isaac's shoulders, while he himself carried the fire and the knife. As the two walked on together, Isaac spoke to his father Abraham: "Father!" he said. "Yes, son," he replied. Isaac continued, "Here are the fire and the wood, but where is the sheep for the holocaust?" "Son," Abraham answered, "God himself will provide the sheep for the holocaust." Then the two continued going forward.

When they came to the place of which God had told him, Abraham built an altar there and arranged the wood on it. Next he tied up his son Isaac, and put him on top of the wood on the altar. Then he reached out and took the knife to slaughter his son. But the Lord's messenger called to him from heaven, "Abraham, Abraham!" "Yes, Lord," he answered. "Do not lay your hand on the boy," said the messenger. "Do not do the least thing to him. I know how devoted you are to God, since you did not withhold from me your own beloved son."

(Genesis 22:1-12)

We can only imagine what Abraham was thinking and feeling as he led his only son to be slaughtered. He did not question God as to why he was commanding this sacrifice; he promptly obeyed. Yet we get a sense when reading this passage that perhaps Abraham — who had a solid relationship with and knowledge of God — somehow knew that God would not have him go through with this sacrifice. His response to Isaac's question about the sheep, "God himself will provide the sheep for the holocaust," was possibly more than an evasive answer to conceal Isaac's ultimate fate. Perhaps Abraham knew, or at least hoped, that God would change his instructions and provide for another sacrifice. In any event, he listened to God and obeyed, even if it meant destroying his son. God responded to Abraham's complete surrender to faith by sparing Isaac's life.

Certainly God does not ask us to put our children in the way of danger. God does not delight in death or suffering, as they are solely the result of sin and the ultimate sign of its existence. Yet this episode still gives us much to reflect upon as fathers. Though we do not purposely put our children in harm's way, danger inevitably comes to them from time to time. Parents have to deal with the suffering their children encounter through illness, injury, or emotional troubles. Some parents experience the unbearable pain of losing a child to death. Abraham reminds us that even in the midst of unfathomable suffering, there is always a purpose, whether we understand it or not.

God himself knows the pain of watching his Son suffer and die — there was no worse tragedy in the history of the world than the passion and death of Jesus Christ. Here was the *perfect* human being — God himself become flesh — whose life was only about love. Jesus did not have an ounce of hate or evil in him. His entire life was about loving, healing, reconciling, restoring what was lost. Yet this perfect person, God's own Son, was arrested, falsely convicted, whipped, beaten, mocked, made to carry a heavy wooden cross through crowded streets while people laughed at him and spit upon him. He was then stripped of his clothes, nailed to that cross and left for dead. No tragedy in the history of the world compares to what happened that day. Yet there was a purpose, and a glorious end, for God took the single most evil event in the history of the world and turned it into the most glorious — the means for all sinners to return to him. Jesus suffered and died so that all of us — for whom he endured that suffering and death — could be reconciled to God. God took the world's worst tragedy and turned it into triumph. He promises to always do the same for the tragedies we experience in our families, whether we see the immediate results or not.

St. Joseph did not live to see his son endure his passion. But Mary, his mother, and God, his Heavenly Father, experienced it all. Whenever we find ourselves struggling to accept any suffering our children may have to endure, we have some solid company from whom to draw support, and a promise that there is ultimately a good purpose to it all.

The story of Abraham and Isaac is an obvious prefiguring

of this sacrifice of Jesus. A loving father is set to sacrifice his only son as a sin offering, making the son carry the wood on which he will be put to death. In this story it is only a test of Abraham's obedience. In Jesus' case the sacrifice was to atone for *our* disobedience. There is no amount of pain or sorrow we will endure as parents that cannot be brought to the cross of Christ to be redeemed. God sacrificed his own Son so that we and our children would not have to suffer into eternity. All human suffering is a participation in this same saving action. As painful as it is to endure, we know that suffering holds a place of honor, for it joins us to the greatest act of love the world has ever known.

Abraham also had an understanding that Isaac was not his possession. Isaac actually belonged to God, Abraham was the steward given the charge of his care. What ultimately happens to Isaac is God's prerogative as his true father, not Abraham's. If God indeed wanted Isaac to be sacrificed, Abraham had no right to interfere with those plans. As fathers we need to have a life that is deeply rooted in prayer and a knowledge of God, for we too are stewards of God's children, and God has plans for them which he will reveal to and through us. We have to be ready to recognize God's revelations to us about our children, and this can only happen when we are in a regular routine of prayer, worship, spiritual reading, and seeking counsel from wise advisors. From the "Father of the Faith," we learn that we all need to be "Fathers of Faith," and faithful stewards of God's children.

Zechariah

Like Abraham and Sarah, Zechariah and his wife Elizabeth were past childbearing years. Elizabeth was also barren. The Gospel of Luke tells us that Zechariah and Elizabeth "were both righteous before God, blamelessly following all the commandments and regulations of the Lord" (Luke 1:6). The angel Gabriel appeared to Zechariah with the incredible news that Elizabeth would conceive a son, whom they were to name John. He would be a child who "will be great before the Lord." Zechariah is told that the boy "shall drink neither wine nor strong drink," that he will "bring back the hearts of fathers to the children and the rebellious to the wisdom of the upright, to make ready for the Lord a people made perfect" (Luke 1:15, 17).

This child, of course, was John the Baptist. Zechariah questioned the angel, doubting that this conception could happen. Because he doubted, Zechariah was struck mute until the events which the angel foretold came to be. When his tongue was finally loosened after he named the child John, Zechariah uttered a beautiful canticle in praise of God, one which is prayed daily in Morning Prayer from the Liturgy of the Hours, the official prayer of the Church.

Not being able to speak, Zechariah had lots of time to listen and to think. Zechariah's inability to speak is a reminder to us as fathers of the need to listen to our children, and to not always be the one talking. We are trained in that discipline when our children are first learning to speak. We have to really concentrate to understand what some of those garbled syllables are supposed to mean. It is merely the beginning of a lifetime discipline of really focusing and listening to our children.

There is a story about a little boy who came in from playing with a neighbor child and told his parents, "Johnny was telling me about where he came from. Where did *I* come from?" Nervously, the parents explained the "facts of life" to the little boy as carefully and as detailed as possible. When they finished the boy replied, "Oh. Johnny came from New York."

Those parents thought they heard what their child had asked them, but they didn't really. The silence of Zechariah serves as an inspiration to us all of learning to really listen to our children.

The angel Gabriel told Zechariah that his son would "bring back the hearts of fathers to the children and the rebellious to the wisdom of the upright, to make ready for the Lord a people made perfect." It is significant that in describing the mission of the forerunner of the Messiah, one of the details includes bringing back the hearts of fathers to children. If this isn't a reminder of the crucial mission all fathers play in preparing the Kingdom of God, I don't know what is. Zechariah obviously did a tremendous job in raising the young man who would prepare the way of the Lord. When we raise our children in the faith, we are doing the same.

The Father in the Parable of the Prodigal Son

In this parable (Luke 15:11-32) Jesus gives us a powerful lesson on fatherhood. Let's reflect on the challenges facing the father in this story.

First, let's recap the parable. A man had two sons. The younger one asked for his share of his inheritance; the father gave it to him, and shortly afterwards he left home. The son soon squandered all of his inheritance on dissolute living, and he found himself in dire need. He got a job feeding pigs, who ate better than he did. He decided to return home to his father — not to rejoin the family, for he didn't feel worthy to be called a son anymore. He would simply ask his father to take him on as a hired hand so at least he could have shelter and food. He planned to tell his father, "I've sinned against Heaven and before you; I'm no longer worthy to be called your son; treat me like one of your hired men." When the father caught sight of the son a long way off, he was filled with compassion. He ran out to welcome his son home with an embrace and a kiss. He called for a feast in celebration of his son's return. Meanwhile, the older son who had always been obedient objected to a party for the wayward son. The father said to the older boy, "My child, you're always with me and everything of mine is yours, but we *had* to celebrate and rejoice — this brother of yours was dead, and has come back to life, he was lost, and has been found!"

When the younger son asked for his inheritance, he basically told his father, "As far as I'm concerned, you're dead. The money I would receive at your death is more important to me than you, so give it to me now so that I may stop living as your son and become my own person." We can only imagine the tremendous pain this caused the father. But his love for his son was so strong, he respected his request and gave him his half of the inheritance. He let him go. The father knew his son was making a foolish decision, and that dire consequences would be the result.

But he had an insight into love which is often very difficult to put into practice. Love is not controlling — it allows people to make their own decisions and to learn from them. This is the way that God treats us. He knows the consequences of our poor decisions even before we make them. Yet he doesn't stop us. He is always there to offer guidance, but he never forces himself on anyone. As God's instrument to our children, we need to have the same attitude.

When the son returned, the father was full of compassion. He didn't even wait for the son to say anything. The mere sight of the son returning down the road was enough for the father to be moved to forgiveness. While the son had written the father off and basically disowned him, the father never disowned the son. Our children are *always* our children, no matter what. We must always welcome them back with open arms.

The father's response to the older son reveals what kind of a father he was, too. On the one hand he has to affirm the older son's place in his heart and in the family. On the other, he has to balance the responsibility the family has to look out for each other, and to stress that a family really is not a family until it is whole. Basically what the father said to the older son was, "You have always had your part in the family, but we weren't a family until your brother came home. Now that we are a family again, we really must celebrate." It was a delicate balance which all fathers must learn to make in loving their children equally.

Jairus

In the Gospel of Mark we read the following story:

When Jesus had again crossed over to the other side a large crowd gathered around him, as he stood by the sea. One of the rulers of the synagogue, Jairus by name, came and, when he saw him, fell at his feet and begged him, saying, "My little daughter is dying; please come lay your hands on her and save her life!" So he went off with him.... Some people came from the ruler of the synagogue's household and said, "Your daughter has died; why trouble the teacher any further?" But Jesus paid no attention to what was being said and told the ruler of the synagogue, "Don't be afraid; just believe!" And he didn't allow anyone to accompany him except Peter and James and James' brother John. When they came to the leader of the synagogue's house Jesus saw the confusion and the people weeping and wailing loudly, and when he entered he said to them, "Why are you upset and weeping? The child hasn't died, she's sleeping!" And they just laughed at him. But after driving them all out he took the father of the child and the mother and those who were with him, and he went in to where the child was; and taking hold of the child's hand he said to her, *"Talitha koum,"* which, translated, is, "Little girl, I say to you, arise!" At once the little girl got up and began to walk around — she was twelve years old. And at once they were completely overcome with amazement. Then he gave strict orders that no one should know of this and said to give her something to cat.   (Mark 5:21-24, 35-43)

As Jairus faced a critical situation with his child, he knew the only thing to do was to put her care completely into Jesus' hands and to trust him entirely. As a leader of the synagogue Jairus answered many people's difficult questions about their life and about God, but he was powerless to do anything for his dying daughter. As parents our natural instinct is to care for our children and to help them through any difficulty. Nothing is more frustrating or heartbreaking than watching our children face a difficulty for which we cannot help them. In those instances we have to turn everything completely over to God. We should give our children to Christ no matter what the circumstances.

Though the situation seemed impossible, Jairus had total faith and trust in Jesus to help. When met with the news of his daughter's death, Jairus is told by Jesus, "Do not fear, only believe." We are told the same thing in our vocation as fathers.

Jesus' command that no one should know about this seems puzzling. Yet this idea of a "messianic secret" is a consistent theme of Mark's Gospel. Jesus performs incredible signs that show his power as God, yet he tells people not to tell anyone about it. The reason is that the people had an expectation of the Messiah as a political ruler who would overthrow the Roman empire with a powerful army. Jesus' true mission as the Messiah was to suffer and die, and people were not ready to hear that yet. That is why he kept his identity as Messiah a secret until he was about to go to Calvary. Our obligation as twenty-first century Christians is somewhat the opposite. Whereas the disciples in the gospels saw supernatural miracles which they had to keep secret, we see ordinary, everyday miracles which we are duty-bound to proclaim to the world. As fathers, we need to begin this proclamation to our families, to see the miracles which happen each day and to celebrate them.

Luigi Beltrame Quattrocchi

On October 21, 2001, Pope John Paul II beatified a married couple, Luigi and Maria Beltrame Quattrocchi. Beatification is a step along the process of canonization as a saint. This was the first time in Church history that a husband and wife were beatified as a couple. The Holy Father saw a tremendous need for married people to have a saintly example to follow and someone to intercede for them. We will learn a little about Luigi, the husband and father who was elevated to this status.

Luigi was born in 1880 and grew up in Urbino, Italy. He received a law degree from La Sapienza University in Rome, and began a successful career which included positions in Italy's Inland Revenue Department, the boards of several banks, and honorary deputy attorney general of the Italian State. In 1905 he married Maria Corsini, a devout Catholic girl from Florence. Though Luigi was well-known for his kindness, honesty and selflessness, he did not have a strong faith when he married Maria. She was a tremendous influence on him spiritually. The two began attending daily Mass together. Eventually the family began to pray the Rosary every evening together, kept a holy hour on the eve of the First Friday every month, participated in night vigil prayer, and consecrated themselves to the Sacred Heart of Jesus.

Luigi and Maria had four children: Filippo, Stefania, Cesare and Enrichetta. Filippo and Cesare became priests, and Stefania became a nun. But perhaps the greatest testimony to the faith of this couple involved the circumstances surrounding the birth of their youngest, Enrichetta. Because of complications during the pregnancy, doctors strongly advised an abortion, so that at least Maria's life could be saved. In those days the possibility of Maria's survival under those circumstances was about five percent. Luigi and Maria refused to have their child aborted. They put all their trust in God. Though the pregnancy was one of suffering and anguish, Enrichetta was born healthy, and Maria survived.

Their family life was never dull. There was always time for sports and vacations, and their house was always open to friend and stranger alike. During World War II they took in many refugees.

After twenty years of marriage, Luigi and Maria decided to forgo marital relations as the ultimate sacrifice to God. They lived this way for twenty-six years. Luigi died in 1951, Maria passed away in 1965.

Luigi and Maria seldom fought in the presence of their children. As Enrichetta recalls, "It is obvious to think that at times they had differences of opinion, but we, their children, were never exposed to these. They solved their problems between themselves through conversation, so that once they came to an agreement, the atmosphere continued to be serene."

Pope John Paul II said this at their beatification ceremony:

Drawing on the word of God and the witness of the saints, this blessed couple lived an ordinary life in an extraordinary way. Among the joys and anxieties of a normal family, they knew how to live an extraordinarily rich spiritual life. At the center of their lives was the daily Eucharist as well as devotion to the Virgin Mary, to whom they prayed every evening with the Rosary, and consultation with wise spiritual directors.... In their life, as in the lives of many other married couples who day after day earnestly fulfill their mission as parents, one can contemplate the sacramental revelation of Christ's love for the Church. ...Like every path to holiness, yours too, dear married couples, is not easy. Every day you face difficulties and trials, in order to be faithful to your vocation, to foster harmony between yourselves and your children, to carry out your mission as parents and participate in social life.... Married and family life can also experience moments of bewilderment. We know how many families in these cases are tempted to discouragement. I am particularly referring to those who are going through the sad event of separation; I am thinking of those who must face illness and those who are suffering the premature death of their spouse or of a child. In these situations, one can bear a great witness to fidelity in love, which is purified by having to pass through the crucible of suffering.

May Luigi Beltrame Quattrocchi serve as a sound example and a powerful intercessor for all of us as Christian fathers.

CHAPTER FIVE

Baptism: The Rite Stuff

A very dear priest I know often asks the following question to those gathered to celebrate an infant baptism: "I know you can all tell me your birthday. But how many of you can tell me the date of your baptism?" Most cannot. His point is that our baptism into the life of the Body of Christ is just as important as the day we began our life outside the womb. The day you begin your relationship with your child — be it the day of their birth or the day of their adoption — is a date you remember and celebrate every year. The day your child begins their relationship with God through his instrument of salvation, the Church, is a momentous one as well. It is a day your family is called to celebrate from the moment of your child's birth or adoption. God gave you your child so that you will be his image to them. Integral to that mission is bringing your child for baptism with the promise to raise them in the faith. Since the rite of baptism of children contains rich material for reflection, I will draw upon its key elements to discuss the importance of your child's baptism, and arranging for this sacrament as early as possible.

As the rite of baptism begins, the priest or deacon asks three questions of the parents. The first two are fairly simple. He asks, "What name do you give your child?" That's an easy one, unless you're incredibly nervous. Yet the question is profound. In the early days of the Church, still deeply rooted in Judaism, the giving of a name was a significant part of giving the child their identity. Often children are named after someone whose life example their parents hope they will emulate. Some psychological research suggests that a person's name plays a significant part in helping to shape their personality. Thus you are not merely being asked the name you have given your child. The rite acknowledges that you have also given your child an identity, and the celebrant asks for it so that your child will be identified with the Church as well. What is being asked is not just, "What is the name," but, "Who is this child you have brought here?"

The second question is, "What do you ask of God's Church for your child?" The water in the font should give that answer away: "Baptism." Yet when we understand what baptism is, again, the question is quite profound. In baptism we are joined to the death of Jesus — we go to the grave with him — so that we can share also in his resurrection. We are permanently, indelibly configured to him, with a mark on our soul that can never be taken away. We are asking that our child die with Jesus in order to rise with him, to be committed to the life of the Church, and we are accepting the promise to share the faith with them and nourish them.

The third question reads as follows: "You have asked to have your children baptized. In doing so you are accepting the responsibility of training them in the practice of the faith. It will be your duty to bring them up to keep God's commandments as Christ taught us, by loving God and our neighbor. Do you clearly understand what you are undertaking?" The rite calls for the parents to respond, "We do." But in reality, we really don't understand the responsibility involved in raising God's children to seek him and to know him. It's something we accept entirely on faith, and will only come to grasp as the years go by.

Celebrating my parents' 50th wedding anniversary drove that point home for me. I thought about the day when these two young twenty-somethings stood before a priest in a church in Chicago and promised to be true to each other in good times and in bad, in sickness and in health, for richer or for poorer, until death. Looking at their wedding pictures I have the perspective of fifty years of hindsight. I know many of the things my parents have had to deal with in their marriage while raising six children — tremendous joys, unbearable heartaches, triumphs and tragedies too numerous to mention. With many of these events in mind, I look at those grainy black and white photographs of these two young kids and think, "They had no idea what they were getting themselves into." They really had only three things that day, now over fifty years in the past: faith, hope and love. They had faith — in God and in each other — that whatever life might bring their way they had God and each other to count on. They had hope for a fulfilling life — not an easy one, but one laden with the wonder of living in union with God through their marital bond. And they had love, which endures all things, bears all things, believes all things, hopes all things.

Just like any ancestor of our faith tradition — Abraham, Moses, Jonah, John the Baptist, St. Peter, among many others

— my parents had no idea what lay in store for them when they accepted the call of God. But they followed, and were richly blessed. As a result, I can pass those blessings on to my children and grandchildren.

The godparents are then asked, "Are you ready to help these parents in their duty as Christian mothers and fathers?" The role of a godparent is sometimes misunderstood; the word itself is misleading. It is a compound word which breaks into "God" and "parent." The person or persons you ask to assume this role are asked to be neither to your child. God will be God; being the parent is your job. In fact, the English translation of the Code of Canon Law — which lists the legal requirements for all the sacraments — purposely replaces the word "godparent" with a term which more accurately describes this role: "sponsor."

As parents we are the ones primarily responsible for raising our children in the faith. Yet the Church community has a vital role to play as well. The godparent represents this broader Church community. By participating in the baptism they are helping to establish this bridge. The people who present the child for baptism are the parents, and a representative (or two) from the Church to symbolize the partnership between parents and Church which is now beginning.

Just like any other organization which requires someone who is already a member to sponsor a new member, godparents at a Catholic baptism must be fully initiated, practicing members of the Catholic faith, at least 16 years of age, and eligible to receive the sacraments themselves. Someone who is not a full, active member in any organization cannot sponsor someone else for membership.

The next element of the baptism rite I would like to draw your attention to is the following litany, which occurs after a brief Liturgy of the Word. In the rite itself this litany is very brief, although the officiating priest or deacon is free to add to it. But it bears some consideration as you either prepare for or reflect upon your own child's baptism. It goes like this:

> Holy Mary, Mother of God, pray for us.
> Saint John the Baptist, pray for us.
> Saint Joseph, pray for us.
> Saint Peter and Saint Paul, pray for us.
> All you saints of God, pray for us.

It is so brief that the significance of this litany can be easily overlooked. But read the last line very carefully: "All you saints of God, pray for us." Literally and truly, that is what is happening at that moment. As your child is preparing to be baptized, all the saints of Heaven are called upon to pray for your child at that very moment. Think of the prayer power that is being called upon there. Think of the tremendous heritage your child is joining. Realize that when your child is baptized it is more than the assembly gathered at your parish church who are participating in this ritual. The *entire Church* from all times and all places are joining you. That's how important this moment is to God, to the Church, and to you.

Next we have a prayer with a somewhat frightening name, the prayer of exorcism. Usually this word conjures up images of Linda Blair in various grotesque expressions in the popular film *The Exorcist*. What this prayer is in the rite of baptism is a prayer for strength for your child to resist the temptation of sin.

Form B of the exorcism prayer reads as follows: "Almighty God, you sent your only Son to rescue us from the slavery of sin, and to give us the freedom only your sons and daughters enjoy. We now pray for these children who will have to face the world with its temptations, and fight the devil in all his cunning. Your Son died and rose again to save us. By his victory over sin and death, cleanse these children from the stain of original sin. Strengthen them with the grace of Christ, and watch over them at every step in life's journey. We ask this through Christ our Lord."

Next comes the first of two anointings with holy oils your child receives. The celebrant says, "We anoint you with the oil of salvation in the name of Christ our Savior; may he strengthen you with his power, who lives and reigns for ever and ever. Amen." The children are then anointed with the Oil of Catechumens. "Catechumen" is an ancient word from the earliest days of the Church which refers to those who are preparing for baptism. Catechumens were adults or older children who spent a period of formation in preparation for their entrance into the Church community. The Church refers to adults and older children preparing for baptism today as catechumens. The word actually means "echo." When we echo, we give something back exactly as we have heard it. The baptized are reminded of their obligation to pass on the faith exactly as they have received it, not to alter it in any way. The Oil of Catechumens is one of two holy oils used in your child's baptism rite. These oils were blessed by your diocesan bishop during Holy Week in preparation for the celebration of the Easter sacraments.

When the water to be used in baptism is blessed, five important events in our salvation history are recalled. The prayer speaks of water at the creation of the world, reminding us that everything that lives needs water. We recall the great flood, where God cleansed the earth of sin and began again with Noah and his family. The flood waters were a precursor of baptism; Noah's ark was a figure for the Church. The Church is the "bark of Christ," and when we enter it we are likewise rescued by the waters of baptism from the destruction caused by sin. The prayer recalls how the Israelites were rescued from the slavery of Egypt by their passing through the waters of the Red Sea. By passing through the waters of baptism, we are freed from our slavery to sin. The prayer recalls Jesus' own baptism by John at the Jordan River. Jesus was sinless, God incarnate; he had no need for baptism. Yet he wanted to be in complete solidarity with the rest of us who do need it. In a sense, being baptized was Jesus' way of showing us that he is the example of what we are to do, and also that he wants to identify with everything about our lives. The prayer recalls that when Jesus' side was pierced on the cross, blood and water flowed out. This was to show that even though Jesus had died, his mission was not to end in death. New life would come about.

The parents and godparents are then once again reminded of the awesome responsibility they are assuming: "Dear parents and godparents: You have come here to present these children for baptism. By water and the Holy Spirit they are to receive the gift of new life from God, who is love. On your part, you must make it your constant care to bring them up in the practice of the faith. See that the divine life which God gives them is kept safe from the poison of sin, to grow always stronger in their hearts."

And then: "If your faith makes you ready to accept this responsibility, renew now the vows of your own baptism. Re-

ject sin, profess your faith in Christ Jesus. This is the faith of
the Church. This is the faith in which these children are about
to be baptized."

The parents and godparents are then asked to renounce sin
by answering "I do" to the following three questions: "Do you
reject Satan? And all his works? And all his empty promises?"

They are then asked to profess their faith by answering "I
do" to the following: "Do you believe in God, the Father almighty, creator of heaven and earth? Do you believe in Jesus
Christ, his only Son, our Lord, who was born of the Virgin Mary,
was crucified, died, and was buried, rose from the dead, and is
now seated at the right hand of the Father? Do you believe in
the Holy Spirit, the holy catholic Church, the communion of
saints, the forgiveness of sins, the resurrection of the body, and
life everlasting?" The celebrant concludes: "This is our faith. This
is the faith of the Church. We are proud to profess it, in Christ
Jesus our Lord."

The child is then baptized, either immersed three times
or by having water poured over the head three times, as the
celebrant says, "I baptize you in the name of the Father and of
the Son and of the Holy Spirit."

Your child is then anointed with the second holy oil —
blessed by your bishop during Holy Week — to be used in this
rite. That is the oil of Chrism. This is a perfumed oil whose name
derives from the same root as "Christ." In ancient times anoint-
ing with oil was used during important ceremonies as the sign
of being given a mission. With Chrism, the Church is reminding us that your child has been marked with the mission of living the life of a Christian. (Chrism is also used in Confirmation
and in ordination to Holy Orders.) The celebrant says, "The God

of power and Father of our Lord Jesus Christ has freed you from sin and brought you to new life through water and the Holy Spirit. He now anoints you with the chrism of salvation, so that, united with his people, you may remain for ever a member of Christ who is Priest, Prophet and King."

The newly baptized are then clothed with a white garment — symbolic of becoming a new creation — with the words, "You have become a new creation, and have clothed yourself in Christ. See in this white garment the outward sign of your Christian dignity. With your family and friends to help you by word and example, bring that dignity unstained into the everlasting life of heaven." The clothing with the white garment is symbolic also of being accepted into a family. Recall Jesus' parable of the prodigal son, who left home, squandered his inheritance, then came back to his father asking only to be taken back as a hired worker. The father was overjoyed, welcomed him back into the family, and called for a robe to be put on him. Your child is promised the same welcome into God's arms when they seek him with a pure heart.

Next, the child is presented with a lighted candle. The celebrant says, "Parents and godparents, this light is entrusted to you to be kept burning brightly. These children of yours have been enlightened by Christ. They are to walk always as children of the light. May they keep the flame of faith alive in their hearts. When the Lord comes, may they go out to meet him with all the saints in the heavenly kingdom."

The very large candle used in the baptism rite has a significant history. It is called the Paschal Candle, Easter Candle, or Christ Candle. If you've ever attended an Easter Vigil liturgy, you know of its significance. If not, allow me to fill you in.

On the evening of Holy Saturday, the night leading into Easter Sunday, the Church celebrates its most sacred, solemn liturgy of the year. This service begins with a fire outside the church, and the Paschal Candle — a brand new one for the year — is blessed. Using a stylus, the celebrant marks the candle and says the following: "Christ yesterday and today, the beginning and the end. Alpha, and Omega; all time belongs to him, and all the ages: to him be glory and power through every age for ever. Amen."

He then takes five nails — reminiscent of the nails driven into Christ's hands and feet and the spear thrust into his side — and pierces them into the candle in the shape of a cross, saying: "By his holy and glorious wounds may Christ our Lord guard us and keep us. Amen."

Lighting the candle with the blessed fire, the celebrant says: "May the light of Christ, rising in glory, dispel the darkness of our hearts and minds."

A solemn procession then begins with this candle, and the symbolism is powerful. The church is in total darkness, with all the lights turned off, while this ceremony has taken place outside the front doors. This symbolizes the darkness that the world has been cast into as the result of sin. The nails going into the candle recall Jesus' passion and death. The lighting of the flame on top of the candle afterwards calls to mind his resurrection, his victory over death. This candle is then brought into the entrance of the church, where it pierces the darkness. The message is powerful: Christ has risen, and it is his light which has come to save this world in darkness.

As the procession continues, the faithful who were gathered around the fire now begin to process into church behind the candle. Everyone is carrying a small candle, taking a light from the Paschal Candle. This reminds us that the more people who accept the light of Christ and are willing to let it shine in their lives, the brighter the world becomes.

This Easter Vigil is when adults are baptized, confirmed and receive Eucharist, and where the baptismal waters for the Easter season are blessed.

You can appreciate why it is helpful to know something about this candle and its place in the baptism ceremony. Because of the Paschal Candle's significance as a primary symbol of the resurrection, there are only certain times in the liturgical life of the Church that it is used: at all Masses during the Easter season, at baptisms and at funerals.

A candle symbolizes many things. Light shines in the darkness to show us the way to go. For the baptized, Jesus is to be this light. A candle gives warmth; for the baptized, Jesus is the source of warmth in a world that often seems cold. As a candle burns it gradually is consumed. The flame remains, but the candle eventually disappears. For the baptized, we are to allow the light of Christ to gradually consume us, so that it is truly Christ working through us and not us acting by ourselves. As John the Baptist stated quite eloquently, "So this my joy has been fulfilled. He must increase while I decrease" (John 3:29-30).

Next comes a prayer called "Ephphatha," an Aramaic word meaning, "Be opened." It comes from the following gospel passage:

When he left the region of Tyre again he went through Sidon to the Sea of Galilee, through the region of the Decapolis. The people there brought him a deaf and tongue-tied man and begged him to lay his hands on him. He took him off alone away from the crowd and put his fingers into his ears, and after spitting he touched his tongue. Then he looked up to Heaven, sighed, and said to him, "Ephphatha," that is, "Be opened!" At once his ears were opened and the knot in his tongue was loosed and he began to speak properly. Jesus ordered them to tell no one, but the more he ordered them all the more did they proclaim it. The people were utterly astonished and said, "Surely he's done everything! He makes the deaf hear and the dumb speak!"   (Mark 7:31-37)

In praying "Be opened," the celebrant touches the child's lips and ears, that they will always be open to listening to God's voice and proclaiming the gospel with their words.

We then pray the prayer which is said at every Catholic liturgy, for it is the one prayer that Jesus himself taught us to pray: "Our Father, who art in heaven, hallowed be thy name. Thy kingdom come, thy will be done, on earth as it is in heaven. Give us this day our daily bread, and forgive us our trespasses, as we forgive those who trespass against us. Lead us not into temptation, but deliver us from evil."

When the disciples asked Jesus how to pray, he gave them the words above. While they are profound for all Christians, they are particularly meaningful for us as fathers, called to reveal and relive the fatherhood of God on earth. We are all united under one Heavenly Father. The last two lines I find particularly relevant for fathers: "Forgive us our trespasses, as we forgive those who trespass against us. And lead us not into temptation, but deliver us from evil." As fathers we are called to be radically forgiving. We must really be on the watch for how forgiving we are of our wives and children, for in this prayer we are asking God to treat us no differently. Setting the example for our children, we need to diligently try to avoid situations which will lead us into temptation, thus to be delivered from evil.

As the baptism rite draws to a close, there is a blessing for the mothers and fathers of the children, as well as to all assembled. I conclude this chapter with those three prayers:

God the Father, through his Son, the Virgin Mary's child, has brought joy to all Christian mothers, as they see the hope of eternal life shine on their children. May he bless the mothers of these children. They now thank God for the gift of their children. May they be one with them in thanking him for ever in heaven, in Christ Jesus our Lord.

God is the giver of all life, human and divine. May he bless the fathers of these children. With their wives they will be the first teachers of their children in the ways of faith. May they also be the best of teachers, bearing witness to the faith by what they say and do, in Christ Jesus our Lord.

By God's gift, through water and the Holy Spirit, we are reborn to everlasting life. In his goodness, may he continue to pour out his blessings upon all present, who are his sons and daughters. May he make them always, wherever they may be, faithful members of his holy people. May he send his peace upon all who are gathered here, in Christ Jesus our Lord.

CHAPTER SIX

Mass Confusion

When you are a parent managing very young children in church, and the priest says, "The Mass is ended, go in peace," the response "Thanks be to God" takes on a whole new meaning!

I am the father of three "energetic" children, and Mass is often an adventure. I can remember a time B.C. (Before Children) when I would arrive for Mass a little early, spend some time in quiet reflection, remain comfortably in my pew, participate attentively, and leave with a sense that I really had encountered God in a wonderful way, truly "going in peace." Nowadays I sometimes spend Mass time going back and forth to the cry room with any combination of my children, walking around the vestibule, showing them the votive candles and statues, or in the case of a severe crying spell (either theirs or mine) taking them outside. Mass with young children can be a full-blown emotional, mental and physical workout. Often I am exhausted afterwards, feeling like I didn't go to Mass at all, and that I received very little out of it. But as hectic and nerve-racking as it can be, my young family attends Mass every week, for some very important reasons.

My children came to know at a very young age that our church is an important place we go every week. It has been part of their weekly routine since they were infants. My kids may not know much about the Church just yet, but they do know that going to Mass is a priority in our family's life. I have had parents of young children tell me that they don't yet bring their children to church because they feel awkward about the disruption they sometimes cause, or that they are waiting until "they enjoy going" so they can attend together as a family. If you're going to wait until your children "enjoy" going to church, you're going to be waiting a very long time. The longer you take to introduce that routine, the harder it will be to begin. As far as the distraction your children may cause at Mass, their disruptions can actually be a powerful ministry to others in the assembly. I will explain that point in a bit.

As unbelievable as it may seem, the youngest of children actually get something out of going to church. Weekly Mass attendance has made quite an impression on my son Zachary. He often plays out some Mass parts at home. I have also been able to use some of his hectic, disruptive time as teaching opportunities. For example, our parish has a replica of Michelangelo's Pieta in front, in which Mary holds the crucified body of Jesus in her arms. One day when Zachary was particularly "enthusiastic" we took a time-out outside. I showed him the statue, and explained that Mary is "Jesus' Mama," and that she holds him in her arms "just like your Mama holds you." He has no idea about Jesus as the Son of God, the Paschal Mystery, the Immaculate Conception, or any of that. But he knows that Jesus and Mary are special people to us, and he knows about their relationship to each other. Real foundations have been laid very simply which will make later faith-building easier.

The Mass contains some natural "attention-grabbers" for children: music, colorful vestments and movements by the priest and liturgical ministers, candles, flowers, and whatever appointments the worship space in your church has to offer. Taking advantage of those can help draw your child into the experience of the liturgy.

As a parent I have gained a new appreciation for the meaning of the word *liturgy*, which actually means "the work of the people." Liturgy with young children is definitely work! But the liturgy is really work for everyone who participates, and the struggles with my young children at Mass help me to appreciate the role of the assembly much more clearly. I would like to share with you some insights into the liturgy I have gained through many excruciating worship experiences with my children.

When people come to Mass it is very tempting to adopt the following attitude: "I've worked hard all week at my job and at home. Mass is *my time* to be spiritually refreshed and renewed. This is the hour of the week when other people will take care of *my* needs. I'm going to sit back and be served." While this recharging of our spiritual batteries is a legitimate need and outcome for all of us attending Mass, if we are going only looking to get something, we won't. We don't come to Mass to be served; we come to serve — *to work* — and it is only through this service that we can truly claim to have participated in the liturgy and have "gotten something out of it."

Jesus has given us many examples of how we are called to serve when we gather together for worship. We will reflect briefly upon two of them. Of all the miracles Jesus performed in his public ministry, only one is recorded in *all four* gospels: the feeding of the five thousand. The obvious prefiguring of the Eucharist in this story is a key reason that all four evangelists saw it important to include in their manuscripts. In setting the stage for the Eucharist which was to come, the following scenario plays out, as told in the Gospel of Matthew:

> Jesus left privately by boat for a desert place, and when the crowds heard where he'd gone they followed him on foot from the cities. When he got out of the boat he saw a large crowd, and he was moved with pity for them and healed their sick. When evening had come his disciples came to him and said, "This is a desert place and the day has already come to a close; send the crowds away so they can go off to the villages and buy themselves some food." But Jesus said to them, "There's no need for them to go away; *you* give them something to eat." They said to him, "We have nothing here except five loaves and two fish." "Bring them here to me," he said. After ordering the crowds to recline on the grass he took the five loaves and the two fish and, looking up to Heaven, he gave a blessing, and after breaking them he gave the loaves to his disciples and his disciples gave them to the crowds. They all ate and were filled, and they picked up what was left of the bread — twelve baskets full.   (Matthew 14:13-20)

In the beginning of this passage Jesus obviously needed to be alone, withdrawing to a deserted place by himself. This is the feeling many people have when coming to church. Yet when the needy crowds followed him, Jesus' reaction was not, "Oh no! I really need a rest, can't they just leave me alone? This is *my* time to be refreshed." Instead he ministered to them in the midst of his own tiredness. Jesus' disciples likewise at the end of the day were looking for a way out of serving these people: "Dismiss the crowds so that they can go to the villages and buy food for themselves." But Jesus told the disciples that *they* were to get to work and feed the crowds. This was not a time for them to sit back and relax; they had to labor in service to others. Jesus provided the miracle, the disciples supplied the physical labor, and together they produced a surplus. Thus everyone's needs were met, and the disciples eventually received their well-deserved rest.

When the time came for Jesus to enter into his passion, he called the twelve apostles to the meal in which he would institute the Eucharist; this was really the first Mass. The following episode related in the Gospel of John set the tone for all future Eucharistic celebrations and their participants:

> Knowing that the Father had given all things into his hands and that he had come from God and was now returning to God, he got up from the banquet and laid aside his cloak, and he took a towel and wrapped it around himself. Then he poured water into the wash-basin and began to wash the disciples' feet and wipe them dry with the towel he'd wrapped around himself.... After he'd washed their feet and had put his cloak back on he sat down again and said to them, "Do you understand what I've done for you? You call

me 'The Teacher' and 'The Lord,' and rightly so, because I am. So if I, the Lord and Teacher, have washed
your feet, you too, ought to wash each others' feet,
because I've given you an example so that, just as I've
done for you, you, too, should do."

(John 13:2b-5, 12-15)

Earlier in his ministry Jesus had told the apostles, "Those
considered rulers among the Gentiles lord it over them, and their
leaders exercise authority over them. But it must not be like that
among you; instead, whoever would be great among you, must
be your servant, and whoever would be first among you, must
be the slave of all; for the Son of Man came, not to be served,
but to serve, and to give his life as a ransom for many" (Mark
10:42-45).

We come to Mass not to sit back and be refreshed, but to
work. We are actively joining ourselves to this celebration, con-
tributing so that this will be a beneficial experience for our brothers and sisters in the pews with us. As parents of young children, we get a unique opportunity to explore insights into this
reality.

The workout we get with our children at Mass is a reminder
of why we are at Mass — not to receive, but to serve. It is
through service, the work of the liturgy, that we receive what
we need. At this point in our lives that work may involve attending to our little ones' needs, and keeping them from dis-
rupting others' experience of the liturgy. Later when we are not
constantly monitoring our children it will mean greeting one
another in a welcoming way, listening attentively to the readings and homily (after having read the day's Scriptures before-

hand), responding enthusiastically with the assembly's parts, joining in the singing, occasionally taking on the service of a liturgical minister (usher, greeter, lector, musician/singer, extraordinary minister of the Eucharist, etc.), and praying for one another.

Another key aspect of "the work of the people" that is liturgy is driven home to us by the experience of dealing with our children's disruptive behavior, one which many of us privately acknowledge but may be hesitant to discuss. As embarrassing and self-conscious as it is to have a disruptive child in church, our children are actually challenging the rest of the assembly to examine their conscience on a crucial issue. Author Scott Hahn describes this topic beautifully in the following excerpts from his book *The Lamb's Supper: The Mass as Heaven on Earth*. It is a reality of the Christian life that Satan is insanely jealous of anyone having a loving relationship with God, and that the closer we get to God, the harder Satan works to lure our thoughts and actions away from what God expects of us. When we gather for Mass, and prepare to receive the true presence of Christ in the Eucharist, it drives Satan crazy, and he works very hard at that point to distract us. Scott Hahn discusses this in a chapter entitled "Worship is Warfare," for we do combat with the forces which would try to separate us from God. This is the context in which he writes the following:

> What is our particular combat during Mass? Maybe it's warding off contempt for the worshipper whose perfume is too strong, or the man who sings the wrong lyrics off-key. Maybe it's holding back our judgment against the parishioner who's skipping out

early. Maybe it's turning the other way when we begin to wonder how low that neckline really goes. Maybe it's fighting off smugness when we hear a homily riddled with grammatical errors. Maybe it's smiling, in an understanding way, at the mom with the screaming baby.

Those are the tough battles. Maybe they're not as romantic as sabers clashing in a faraway desert, or marching through tear gas to protest injustice. But because they're so perfectly hidden, so *interior*, they require greater heroism. No one but God and His angels will notice that you didn't mentally critique Father's homily this week. No one but God and His angels will notice that you withheld judgment against the family that was underdressed. So you don't get a medal; you win a battle instead....

Think about it: if we all persevere together, you and I will share a home forever with Christ — *with the parishioners we worship beside today.*

Does that make you feel uncomfortable? Maybe you suddenly remembered the parishioners who most get on your nerves. (I know I did.) Could heaven really be heaven if all of our neighbors are there? Could heaven be paradise if Father So-and-So makes it, too? That's the *only* sort of heaven we should think about. Remember, we're a family of the ancient sort: a clan, a tribe. We're all in this together. That doesn't mean we'll always *feel* affection for the people we see at Mass. It does mean we must love them, bear with their weaknesses, and serve them — because they, too, have been identified with Christ. We cannot love Him without loving them. Loving difficult people will refine us. Perhaps only in heaven will our love be so perfected that we can actually *like* these people, too.

I know the self-consciousness of having noisy children at Mass, and the feeling that everyone is looking at us. I often cringe to wonder what people might be thinking of us, or that someone may be annoyed that my children are ruining their experience of liturgy. But I know that I am trying my best to teach my children about worship and what it means to us, that most of the time their behavior is laudable, and that when it is not I do my best to take care of things. If anyone is thinking ill of me or my family, it is really not my problem; it is theirs. My children sometimes give other worshippers the occasion to examine their conscience in the manner described by Dr. Hahn. While I can try to control what my children do or don't do at Mass, I can't control what people will think. It is my hope that anyone who is annoyed by my children's occasional outbursts may come to some fruitful spiritual insight as a result.

A quote from Charles Dickens' *A Christmas Carol* comes to mind. Returning home from Christmas morning church services with his crippled son Tiny Tim, Bob Cratchit tells his wife, "Somehow he gets thoughtful, sitting by himself so much, and thinks the strangest things you ever heard. He told me, coming home, that he hoped the people saw him in the church, because he was a cripple, and it might be pleasant to them to remember upon Christmas Day, who made lame beggars walk, and blind men see." Often the uncomfortable things we observe — in church or anywhere — have a way of turning our thoughts to the Lord if our dispositions are correct.

Quite frankly, a church without crying children is a church without a future. As the title of Scott Hahn's book implies, Mass is truly Heaven on earth, when Heaven touches down upon earth and we are actually there. Who deserves to be there more than children, whom Jesus beckoned to come to him? It is much better to spend Mass in the cry room than to not go at all. As we read in the Gospel of Matthew: "Then children were brought to him so he could lay his hands on them and pray, but the disciples rebuked him. Jesus said, 'Let the children be, and don't stop them from coming to me, for of such as these is the Kingdom of Heaven!'" (Matthew 19:13-14).

Before my family leaves for church we always make sure we have the necessary "survival tools." These include books, *quiet* toys, drinks (for the kids, not for us), and some kind of crackers or cereal for them to eat. Having something to eat is often the only way to keep young children calm in church. Do they have an intuitive appreciation for the Eucharist and the significance of food in this sacred place? Think about it. Food and drink are a natural comfort not only for children, but for adults as well. That's why Jesus gave himself to us in his most intimate way under the form of food and drink. This is no coincidence. Thus feeding crackers and juice to your child at Mass can be much more than a simple attempt to keep them quiet so as not to disturb others' reflection; it can be a powerful source of reflection for *you*. They are being physically comforted by that food and drink very much like the way *you* will be spiritually comforted by the food and drink you will receive from the altar later in the Mass. Think about that the next time your child is munching and slurping away. I recall one time when Zachary tried to offer me one of his crackers at Mass. Observing the fasting regulation, I politely turned him down. This was not good enough for him, however, and he continued to try to force the cracker into my mouth, as I continued to playfully resist. It was really a Eucharistic moment. My son was being satisfied by his food, and he wanted to share it with me. Instead of being annoyed by his attempt to force a cracker into my mouth at Mass, I saw it as a blessing of Eucharistic love, a sign from God of the much better food I was about to receive.

Even the most disastrous incidents at Mass can become sources of reflection. One weekend my two-year-old daughter Elizabeth slipped off the pew and hit her head on the corner of the hymnal rack. I quickly snatched her up and brought her to the vestibule; when I got there I saw that her face was covered in blood. It is a frightening moment for a parent when your child is bleeding profusely and you do not yet know the location or the extent of the cut. Fortunately, I was soon able to clean enough blood off her face to discover that she had a small cut on her forehead, not nearly as serious as the amount of blood would suggest. As wrenching as those moments are when we see our children suffer, it must be merely the smallest glimpse into what God experienced when his only Son went to the cross to shed his blood for the salvation of the world. We were not able to stay for the rest of Mass, as we had to leave to tend to her wound. While we were not able to participate in the sacrifice of the Body and Blood of Christ on that day, my daughter's spilled blood still turned my attention to the passion, and my appreciation for it.

Phyllis Chandler and Joan Burney offer the following advice in dealing with our children at church:

If Mass is an unpleasant experience for a small child, it can be harmful to the child's developing attitudes towards religion.

The most important thing your child can experience in church is love. We come together in Eucharist to celebrate God's love for us. Your child learns about God's love through your love, which she sees and feels. This love, ever present, should be communicated very clearly in church, God's place.

To many small children the experience of going to church means reminders to sit still, threats of punishment, scowls and angry looks, sometimes even shakes, pokes, and slaps. It should be no surprise that children who endure such experiences do not look forward to going to church and frequently quit going as soon as they have a choice.

Developing some kind of family prayer life at home is also important. Even a simple prayer before meals and at bedtime can go a long way in laying the foundation for a spiritual life in your child. Again, even at a very young age, my children recognize that there is a connection between the prayers we say at home and what we do at church. The sign of the cross is a powerful gesture which helps to bridge home and church. Any other elements of liturgy you can incorporate into your prayer at home will continue to reinforce that relationship.

Another key element of instilling a sense of the sacred in young children is religious art around the house. The more exposure they have to pictures of Jesus, Mary and the saints, and other images of our faith, the easier it is to fit prayer and a growing faith development into their lives. In addition to traditional religious objects, it is very important to develop a sense of the sacredness of ordinary household objects. This helps our children learn that faith is not just something that comes to life when we attend church services or when we have formal prayer time at home; but it is alive in everything we do. A small, personal example I can offer is the mug I use to drink my coffee every morning. When my daughter Elizabeth was born the hospital left a "goodie bag" in the birthing units for the families. Ours included a Noah's Ark coffee mug. I have taken my coffee from that mug almost every morning since. The fact that the picture of Noah's Ark is a religious one is beside the point. That mug is sacred to me because it is a reminder of the birth of my daughter. My kids know where that mug came from and why it is important to me. It is helping them to develop a sense of the sacred in our family life.

Another example is a small gift I am planning to make to each of my children on their eighteenth birthdays. I got the idea when my oldest child was born. That was quite a hectic night into day. We left for the hospital at 2:15 AM and he was born at 4:43 PM. I went to the hospital wearing the shirt I was sleeping in when my wife woke me to let me know it was time to go: a Baltimore Orioles tee shirt. I spent the next 14 1/2 hours in that shirt watching and waiting through the excruciating labor my wife went through, and it is what I was wearing when I first laid eyes on my son. When I was finally able to change out of it I decided that I would wash it and then "retire" it — never wear it again — out of respect for the sacredness of the event I had worn it for. It will never be worn by anyone again until I give it to my son on his eighteenth birthday and tell him the story of his birth and the sacredness of that shirt. I am doing the same for each of my children.

Author Tom McGrath writes the following on this topic:

> Being a parent gives you daily opportunities to experience life at sacred depths. Think of the parent holding the little teddy bear that belonged to the child who died young. Imagine the dad who takes his coffee break using the "World's Greatest Dad" mug he got from the stepchild who had greeted him with such suspicion and hostility just years before. Think of the mom who straightens her son's room and always gives an extra bit of care to the speech trophy won by a boy who found the grace to overcome his terrifying shyness. Our lives are filled with sacred objects. St. Benedict told his monks to treat all household items as if they were vessels of the altar. They are. They bear Christ to us just as surely as the paten and the chalice bear Christ to us on Sunday.

So bring them to church, and make your home a church as well.

CHAPTER SEVEN

Balancing Act

My child arrived just the other day,
He came to the world in the usual way.
But there were planes to catch, and bills to pay.
He learned to walk while I was away.
And he was talking 'fore I knew it, and as he grew,
He'd say, "I'm gonna be like you, Dad.
You know I'm gonna be like you."

So begins Harry Chapin's classic ballad *Cat's in the Cradle*. The story unfolds as presented above. A son wants his father's attention, but his father is too preoccupied with the other responsibilities of life to spend time with him. Yet the boy still looks to him longingly and says, "I'm gonna be like you, Dad." When the son is grown and the retired father finally has time to spend with him, the son is too busy to see him — he has indeed become just like his father.

This song has served as a wise warning to fathers ever since its release in 1974; its message bears repeating here. We have a lot to balance in our lives: our roles as father, husband, employee, parishioner, citizen, son, brother, friend, and the many other roles we each have to play. We have many people to take care of; we also need to take care of ourselves. Striking a proper balance is required, but so difficult.

Perhaps "balance" is an inappropriate word here. Balance implies that everything in our lives is of equal priority, and that we need to devote equal amounts of time and attention to each of them. But in fact this is not the reality. Certain things are more important than others and must take priority. Our relationship with God and our relationship with our family top the list. "Balance" for us means taking care of first things first, and letting everything else in our lives fall into their proper place.

Perhaps you have heard of or seen the following demonstration. When I first heard of this it was in the context of a professor at a business school giving a lecture on time management. The teacher filled a bucket to the brim with fist-sized rocks and showed it to the class asking, "Is this bucket full?" The students responded, "Yes." The professor asked, "Are you sure?" He then poured a bag of gravel into the bucket, and the gravel filled in the spaces between the rocks. The teacher asked, "Now is the bucket full?" The class had caught on that the professor was up to something, so they responded, "Probably not." The teacher then poured sand in the bucket, and the sand filled in the spaces between the gravel. After asking again if the bucket is full, the teacher added water, which filled up the space between the grains of sand until the bucket was finally full.

The professor then asked the class, "What do you think was the purpose of this demonstration?" As ambitious business students attending a lecture on time management, they answered, "No matter how busy our schedules become, there is always room for something else." The teacher replied, "No, that is not the point at all. The point is that unless you put the big rocks in first, they will never get in."

The principle of this little demonstration says a lot to us as fathers. We have many different things competing for space in our buckets. We have to make sure the "big rocks" go in first. Otherwise smaller things will take the place of what rightly belongs there. When we focus on the "big rocks," we may learn that perhaps the gravel and the sand and the water were not as important as we once thought, and we can really do without them.

Obviously the biggest rocks are a relationship with God and whatever nourishes and strengthens it, and our relationship with our family. Interestingly enough, the image of rocks is used throughout Scripture in a variety of contexts to help us understand the various dimensions of our relationship with God. The following reflections on six of those dimensions may be of help to you as you put the "big rocks" in your own bucket.

Laying the Cornerstone

> Open the gates of victory; I will enter and thank the Lord. This is the Lord's own gate, where the victors enter. I thank you for you answered me; you have been my savior. The stone the builders rejected has become the cornerstone. By the Lord has this been done; it is wonderful in our eyes. This is the day the Lord has made; let us rejoice in it and be glad.
>
> (Psalm 118:19-24)

The cornerstone is but one piece of an arch, but without it the rest cannot stand. The cornerstone, once laid in its proper position, makes the arch a whole. Our relationship with God may likewise seem to be just one piece of our lives. But even if we put it first — at the very top of our priorities — if we consider it just *one piece*, then we won't become whole. We can't have a "spiritual side" and other various "sides" to our being, for Jesus told us we cannot serve two masters, and that a house divided against itself will fall. We have to learn to consider *everything* in our lives an experience of God, and to look for him everywhere and in everything. We must see our family as the *primary way* we experience God, and everything else in our lives must be ordered towards that. When we truly make God the cornerstone of our lives — and our family the foundation — everything else will blend into a spiritual whole.

Laying Down the Law

> The Lord said to Moses, "Come up to me on the mountain and, while you are there, I will give you the stone tablets on which I have written the commandments intended for their instruction."
>
> (Exodus 24:12)

The laws of God are carved in stone, but God seeks to place them in our hearts. God wants us to follow his ways not out of a sense of fear or obligation, but from true love and desire. It should be the same in our families. Our children need to look to us not with a sense of fear or obligation, but with a sense of true love based on a knowledge of what family really is. We impart that by welcoming God's law into our hearts and loving and embracing it by the example of our lives. We need to strive to understand God's law more and more so that we know why it is the best way to follow, and to share that with our children.

Stumbling Blocks

> God commands the angels to guard you in all your ways. With their hands they shall support you, lest you strike your foot against a stone. (Psalm 91:11-12)

Our feet will strike against many stones when we follow God in the vocation of fatherhood. Following Jesus in general involves being hurt; fatherhood has its share of unique pains. When we follow the call to love, we make ourselves vulnerable. If fatherhood truly means "playing God," then we are certainly not immune to the suffering God himself accepted when begetting his only Son. Jesus accepted suffering as central to his mission. This is the nature of love. We are hurt so that our wounds, like those of our Lord, can become the source of healing for others. God doesn't always protect us from hurts, but he can guide us to avoid some of them and comforts us in times of pain.

True Food

> After fasting for forty days and forty nights he at last became hungry, and the Tempter approached him and said, "If you're the Son of God, tell these stones to become loaves of bread." But in answer Jesus said,

"Not by bread alone shall man live, but by every utterance proceeding from the mouth of God."

(Matthew 4:2-4)

In each of our lives as fathers there are certain stones which we would rather have turned into something more pleasant. Bread in the desert would be much more satisfying than stones. But we must accept those stones as they are, trusting in God that they are there for a purpose. We need not fear either the stones or those who would tempt us to change them if we truly trust in God.

No More Barriers

Very early in the morning of the first day of the week they came to the tomb when the sun had risen. They were saying to each other, "Who will roll the stone away from the door of the tomb for us?" But when they looked up they saw that the stone had been rolled away, for it was very large.   (Mark 16:2-4)

The huge stone which seemed to separate the women from Jesus had been rolled away. He was changed. He had gone beyond the limits they perceived he had and went beyond their wildest expectations. Often we tend to not give God enough credit for what he can do. We need to call on him for his help and strength, confident that he will go beyond any limits we may have perceived and that nothing can ever stand in our way of becoming the fathers we are called to be.

We Are the Foundation of Our Family

> Jesus asked them, "But who do *you* say that I am?"
> Simon Peter replied, "You're the Messiah, the Son of
> the Living God." In response Jesus said to him,
> "Blessed are you, Simon bar Jonah, for it wasn't flesh
> and blood that revealed this to you, but my Father in
> Heaven. And now I tell you, that you are Peter, and
> on this rock I will build my Church, and the gates of
> hell will not prevail against it. I will give you the keys
> to the Kingdom of Heaven, and whatever you bind
> on earth will have been bound in Heaven, and what-
> ever you loose on earth will have been loosed in
> Heaven." (Matthew 16:15-19)

Peter is the rock upon whom Christ builds his Church. We
are the rock upon whom Christ builds our domestic church, our
family. We are all very different stones of different shapes, sizes
and colors. Often we don't fit together perfectly, but we fit to
form a strong edifice despite the cracks we leave in the struc-
ture. Jesus sent out only eleven very feeble men to change the
world with his help — and they did. We can do the same.

When looking at the many demands on our time and en-
ergy, and wondering if we truly do have the time to give to the
"big rocks" in our bucket, the following Scripture passage can
be very reassuring. Like the lyrics I quoted to open this chapter, this passage was the inspiration for another popular song,
The Byrds' 1960's hit "Turn, Turn, Turn." Take a moment to
read this passage carefully and prayerfully.

There is an appointed time for everything, and a time for every affair under the heavens. A time to be born, and a time to die; a time to plant, and a time to up-root the plant. A time to kill, and a time to heal; a time to tear down, and a time to build. A time to weep, and a time to laugh; a time to mourn, and a time to dance. A time to scatter stones, and a time to gather them; a time to embrace, and a time to be far from embraces. A time to seek, and a time to lose; a time to keep, and a time to cast away. A time to rend, and a time to sew; a time to be silent, and a time to speak. A time to love, and a time to hate; a time of war, and a time of peace. What advantage has the worker from his toil? I have considered the task which God has appointed for men to be busied about. He has made everything appropriate to its time, and has put the timeless into their hearts, without men's ever discovering, from beginning to end, the work which God has done. I recognized that there is nothing bet-ter than to be glad and to do well during life.

(Ecclesiastes 3:1-12)

The reassuring point in this passage is that *there is a time for every affair under the heavens.* God ensures that we have the time to accomplish everything he has called us to do, as long as we manage that time properly. God has "made everything ap-propriate to its time, and has put the timeless into their hearts, without men's ever discovering, from beginning to end, the work which God has done." The demands of the affairs under the heavens seem many and overwhelming. But if God has truly called us to accomplish these things, he will be sure we have the time and resources.

A pastor of mine once made a very wise observation about time in response to the unexpected death of a young person. He said that when someone dies at a young age, people often will say, "Why did he have to die so young, when he had so much more to accomplish?" Yet God, who is present in the past, present and future, knows the number of our days on earth. When we are born, God already knows when we are going to die. Why would God put someone on this earth with a mission to accomplish and not give him the time to fulfill it? God knew this person would die after not too many years on this earth. Would not God have then made it possible for this person to accomplish in those brief years all that he created him to do? There is an appointed time for everything, whether we see it or not. Trusting in God frees us of the worry of whether there will be enough time so we can accept that there is and go about the business of living the life he gave us.

Author Mitch Finley offers the following observation on some of the gravel, sand and water which enters our buckets in his book *For Men Only: Strategies for Living Catholic:*

> Sexual infidelity is, in fact, far from the most common way in which men violate their marriage vows. A man can commit "adultery" with his golf game or sports programs on television. For a Catholic married man who takes his baptism seriously, marital fidelity means making his marriage the top priority in his life. His marriage deserves time and energy, just as his work gets his time and energy. If work comes between

husband and wife for an extended period, then work may become a false God, and nothing will kill a marriage, or a faith, faster than idol worship. Sacrifices may need to be made for the sake of a marriage, and sometimes those sacrifices are professional or financial.

Perhaps each of us needs to take an inventory of the things in our life which take our time and attention and prioritize them to be sure we are really putting first things first.

I have found that simply playing with my children helps me to maintain a sense of balance. Repeating a gospel quote I offered in the first chapter: "Jesus called a child over, placed it in their midst, and said, 'Amen, I say to you, unless you turn and become like children, you won't ever enter the Kingdom of Heaven! Therefore, whoever humbles himself like this child, he's the greatest in the Kingdom of Heaven. And whoever receives one such child in my name, receives me'" (Matthew 18:3-5). Balancing becomes difficult when we try to see too much of the broad picture. When we think about *all* of our responsibilities to care for our children, all of their needs — financial, physical, emotional, spiritual, psychological, social — it is much easier to become stressed. When we can focus instead on one thing at a time, confident that God will give us the time and ability to meet all of these needs in their time, we can relax and be more effective. Again, I have found playing with my children, and really entering into that experience and focusing on their play and their joy, to be the best way to become grounded. My other cares vanish as I see what this is really all about.

In her book *A Simple Path*, Mother Teresa offered the following path to holiness, which stresses a proper balance of the following elements: prayer, faith, love, service, and peace. She describes their relationship as follows: "The fruit of silence is prayer. The fruit of prayer is faith. The fruit of faith is love. The fruit of love is service. The fruit of service is peace." Keeping these elements in balance, and in that order, suggests Mother Teresa, will bring us all peace. I conclude this chapter with the following prayer for families she offers in that same book:

> Heavenly Father, You have given us a model of life in the Holy Family of Nazareth. Help us, O loving Father, to make our family another Nazareth where love, peace and joy reign. May it be deeply contemplative, intensely Eucharistic, and vibrant with joy. Help us to stay together in joy and sorrow through family prayer. Teach us to see Jesus in the members of our family, especially in His distressing disguises. May the Eucharistic Heart of Jesus make our hearts meek and humble like His and help us to carry out our family duties in a holy way. May we love one another as God loves each one of us more and more each day, and forgive each other's faults as you forgive our sins. Help us, O loving Father, to take whatever You give and to give whatever You take with a big smile. Immaculate Heart of Mary, cause of our joy, pray for us. Holy Guardian Angels be always with us, guide and protect us. Amen.

CHAPTER EIGHT

The Many Faces of Fatherhood

Until this point our discussion has focused on a "traditional" model of fatherhood. Yet we know that there are other realities which shape the face of this vocation. Many fathers become so not through birth, but through adoption. Some fathers face the pain of divorce, and the challenge of living their fatherhood without daily contact with their children, and without their children's mother at their side. Others face the tragedy of death — of either their spouse or their child — and continue their life journey missing that essential part of themselves. This chapter will offer some reflections on each of these realities, the "other faces" of fatherhood.

Adoption

The choice to adopt a child is a praiseworthy and blessed one. When a child, through no fault of their own, is for whatever reason deprived of their biological parents, it is the love and dedication of adoptive parents which truly brings them to life and images the love of God. In fact, adoption is used by St.

Paul as a primary image to describe God's relationship to his children. Consider the following excerpts from his letters:

> We know that all creation has been groaning in labor pains up till the present; moreover, we ourselves who have the Spirit as the first fruits are also groaning within ourselves as we await our adoption as sons, the redemption of our bodies.   (Romans 8:22-23)

> They are Israelites, and to them belonged the adoption as sons, the glory of God's presence, the covenants, the giving of the Torah, the Temple worship, and the promises; theirs were the patriarchs, and from them came the Messiah according to the flesh.
> (Romans 9:4-5)

> Blessed be the God and Father of our Lord Jesus Christ who has blessed us in Christ with every spiritual blessing in the heavens. He chose us in Christ before the foundation of the world to be holy and blameless before him. In his love he destined us beforehand to be his adopted sons through Jesus Christ, according to the purpose and desire of his will, to the praise of the glorious grace he bestowed upon us in his Beloved.   (Ephesians 1:3-6)

In the first excerpt from Romans, we have both the images of the labor pains of natural birth, and the wait for adoption. As God's children, we are both his "biological" and "adopted" children. God made us, we came directly from his creative hands and were made in his image and likeness. Yet as the human race we forsake our place in his family by turning to sin instead of to his guidance. (As the prodigal son chose to resign his membership in his family to pursue his own ambitions; see Luke 15:11-32.) Like the prodigal son we seek to return to our Father, but we realize that we in fact left the family. (The prodigal son did not see himself worthy to be re-admitted to his family; he asked his father to simply take him on as one of his hired hands.) Thus the labor pains which St. Paul says are being experienced by all of creation are symptomatic of what the author of Genesis told us — our sinful condition. Looking to be "re-born" into the image of God is a painful one when we have so much sin to overcome. But God is waiting to "adopt" us into a new family — not really new in the sense that we are returning to our same Father and into communion with our brothers and sisters — but new in the sense that this family will not operate under the same conditions as before. St. Paul uses the image of adoption as a powerful description of love. God sees children orphaned by sin and in need of fatherly care, and he takes us unto himself. This is the image which adoptive fathers give to their children, of a God whose compassion would not allow any child to go without parental care, no matter what their circumstances. It is a noble image that needs to be encouraged and supported.

Divorce

One of the most misunderstood Catholic teachings in regards to marriage has to do with divorce. The ending of a relationship is painful enough; often that pain is compounded by a misunderstanding of a divorced person's place in the Church. I would like to offer some insight into the Church's position on this painful issue, and a divorced person's place in the Church. To do this, we need to take a careful look at the meaning of sacramental marriage.

God established the marriage covenant as a revelation of his own covenant with his people. Marriage is used throughout Scripture as a primary image of God's love: *On that day, says the Lord, you will call me, "My husband," and no longer will you call me, "My Baal." I will take you for my wife forever* (Hosea 2:16, 19). *As a young man marries a young woman, so shall your builder marry you, and as the bridegroom rejoices over the bride, so shall your God rejoice over you* (Isaiah 62:5). Basically, God created marriage to be a living sign of his covenant with his people. Husbands and wives are called to love each other as God loves, witnessing the love of God to each other and to the world. A *civil* marriage is the union of two people in a legal covenant. A *sacramental* marriage is the union of two people in the very love of God, who, *as part of the sacrament, works through them as his human instruments*. In a sacramental marriage a husband and wife give themselves to each other to be the primary instrument through which they will experience the love of God. In Catholic sacramental theology, the priest does not confer the sacrament of marriage — the bride and groom bestow it upon each other through the gift of their total person to one another. By declaring a marriage sacramental, the Church is proclaiming that, as far as it can see, God has joined these two people through their mutual self-giving in his own unbreakable bond of love, to be that love to each other.

If we hold this to be true, then we believe that the marriage covenant is by definition graced with the same characteristics of God's covenant with us: it is total, unconditional, intimate, self-sacrificing, forgiving, physically expressed, life-giving, and, above all, permanent. The Catholic Church can never teach that God may one day take back his love from us. As St. Paul writes, "God's gifts and his calling are irrevocable" (Romans 11:29). If we are faithful to the scriptural teaching that marriage is a living sign of God's covenant with his people, then we cannot possibly teach that this covenant can come to an end.

Yet we realize that due to several factors involving human frailty, many marriage relationships do not last. The underlying reason a marriage ends is that one or both of the partners did not love the other the way God loves. If the Church were to regard such unions as sacramental, then we would necessarily be stating that God's covenant with us can also end. A couple is told on their wedding day that they are giving themselves to each other as the principal instrument through which God will love them. What could be more hurtful than telling someone whose marriage relationship has come to an end that God has also broken his covenant, and that this is how God loves and treats them? Yet that is exactly what we would be saying if the sacramental aspect of a marriage were simply declared "ended" as well.

What the Church will do in such instances, out of pastoral love for persons hurting from a broken marital relationship, is to declare that while a *civil marriage* did exist and was brought to an end, the *sacramental grace of God* necessary to preserve the union for life was never established in the first place. This is called an annulment. Again, in Catholic sacramental theology, the priest does not confer the sacrament of marriage — the bride and groom bestow it upon each other through the gift of their

107

total person to each other. While with every wedding the presumption is that the gift is truly being given, sometimes a person only appears to present the gift, when in reality they are not really capable of doing so.

An analogy may be helpful. Suppose I give you a gift for your birthday, but at some time later I take the gift back; perhaps I want to give it to another, or I just want it for myself. What appeared awhile ago to be a gift, in reality turned out to be not a gift at all. A gift is given freely, with no conditions attached, with the giver relinquishing all ownership and attachment to the gift, solely for the good of the other person. If I take my gift back awhile later, then it was never really a gift at all, even though it appeared to be at one time. It turns out that I did not have the proper dispositions to make the gift in the first place.

Recall the insight I shared in Chapter One about the priest whose goal it was to "become a priest." "Becoming married" is also something that takes a lifetime of work. One never finishes "becoming married" until death — in marriage the partners promise to love and honor each other until death do they part. Anything short of that really is not marriage, for one does not "become married" until they have finished that pledge.

When the Church issues a statement of nullity for a marriage, it is saying to the partners, "What you experienced in that relationship is *not* how God loves you! God loves you infinitely more than that! God wants you to be whole and happy, not abandoned and hurt." By declaring an apparently sacramental marriage null, the Church is freeing and healing the partners from an experience that did not truly reflect God's love for them, so that they may be open to knowing his love in a real way. Jesus gave the Church the authority as his instrument that what it declares bound or loosed on earth will be so in heaven (Matthew 16:19). If the Church formally declares a marriage union as sacramental, and later it is proven that it was not, then the Church is duty bound to formally declare it null as well. By definition, the Church cannot declare another marriage union as sacramental until any prior divorced marriages are declared null.

The annulment process can be a painful one; it calls the person seeking the annulment to closely examine the failed relationship. Yet it helps them discover what went wrong, what they can learn from it, and offers them some closure to a painful experience so that they are free to get on with their life and continue to seek God's love and compassionate healing. Understood properly, it is a marvelous sign of God's love.

Any Catholic who has experienced a divorce is welcome with open arms into the Church community. They are encouraged to pursue the painful yet healing annulment process. For the reasons stated above, a divorced Catholic may not enter into a sacramental union with another until their prior union has been declared null. If a divorced Catholic enters into marriage without having their prior marriage annulled, they are breaking communion with the sacramental system of the Church, and have therefore separated themselves from it. They are not eligible to receive any of the sacraments until they get their marriage situation cleared up by the proper Church authorities. Again, a divorced Catholic who remarries without an annulment breaks communion with the Church, *not vice versa*. The Church eagerly awaits their return to communion by following their sacramental obligations.

Given that background, a common question asked by divorced parents seeking an annulment is, "If an annulment states that we were never really married, then are my children illegitimate in the eyes of the Church?" Fr. Joseph M. Champlin offers the following answer to this question:

> No. The parents, now divorced, presumably once obtained a civil license and entered upon a legal marriage. Children from that union are, therefore, their legitimate offspring. *Legitimate* means "legal." The civil divorce and the Church annulment do not alter this situation. Nor do they change the parents' responsibility towards the children. In fact, during annulment procedures the Church reminds petitioners of their moral obligation to provide for the proper upbringing of their children.

God knows what it feels like to be alone. When Jesus endured his worst suffering on the cross at Calvary he uttered these words from Psalm 22: "My God, my God, why have you abandoned me?" Breaking the relationship with the one who was supposed to love us as God loves can bring the same question. Yet that Psalm, while expressing much pain and despair, eventually concludes with the recognition that God really is with his suffering children: "For God has not spurned or disdained the misery of this poor wretch, did not turn away from me, but heard me when I cried out. I will offer praise in the great assembly, my vows I will fulfill before those who fear him. The poor will eat their fill; those who seek the Lord will offer praise" (Psalm 22:25-27).

Death

Death is one thing fathers never want to have to deal with, but unfortunately some do. God also knows that pain — he watched his only Son put to death by violent people. True, he had the advantage of being God, and having complete knowledge of how that situation would turn out. But God knows the pain of death and what it means to his people, and he offers consolation to help us through it. Jesus himself, truly God and truly human, wept at the death of his friend Lazarus. In fact, when Jesus learned that Lazarus was ill, he purposely waited to see him until he knew that he had died (John 11:5-6). Jesus already knew a reality about death that we accept intellectually but often find so difficult to accept in our hearts — that death in Christ is not an end in itself, but results in everlasting life. Jesus allowed Lazarus to die so that the greater glory of God could be shown through his death.

The Gospel of Luke relates the following story which offers a wealth of reflection for anyone mourning the death of a loved one: "On the first day of the week, at early dawn, the women came to the tomb bringing the aromatic spices they had prepared. They found the stone rolled away from the tomb and when they went in they didn't find the Lord Jesus' body, and it happened that when they were at a loss over this, behold, two men in dazzling clothes stood near them. The women were terrified and bowed their faces to the ground, and the men said to them, 'Why are you looking for He Who Lives among the dead?'" (Luke 24:1-5).

I gained a beautiful insight on this passage one day while taking a walk through a cemetery. (I discovered cemeteries to be unique places for reflection one summer when I had a job cutting grass in one. With nothing to do all day but steer a rider mower around headstones, I often found myself reading the names, curious to see what age the people were when they died, when they lived, if they were buried with family, etc. I was always humbled by the realization that every one of those stones represented a person who was given life by God, who walked this earth, had a life, family, friends, talents that they shared, etc. Ever since then I've always found cemeteries quite interesting and great places for thought and reflection.)

On this particular day when I was strolling through a cemetery, for some reason I suddenly looked up at the sky, and doing so stopped me right in my tracks. What a dramatic contrast to where my attention had been previously focused. I was struck by the seemingly infinite majesty of the sky above, and how huge it was compared to this small plot of land I was traversing. Until that point my attention had been focused downwards on the headstones, contemplating only what had been lost. Looking up at the sky made me focus instead on all that is to be gained. It may have been a simple experience, but it changed my outlook drastically. (It was something I never could have done while driving a lawn mower around a cemetery!) I encourage you to try it yourself — take a walk through a cemetery sometime looking at the headstones. Then, after awhile, look up. It will really alter your perspective.

Perhaps the words of the "two men in dazzling clothes" to the women at Jesus' tomb were also being spoken to me that day: "Why do you seek He Who Lives among the dead?" For all who pass the bounds of earth united to the Paschal Mystery of Jesus Christ are not dead, but alive. They are not lost, but have been found, dwelling not in graves, but in the mansions of heaven.

In all four gospel accounts of Easter morning, Jesus' resurrection is not witnessed by anyone. When visitors arrive at the grave, Jesus is already gone. They encounter the *empty tomb*, which becomes the first evidence of the resurrection. As such, it provides rich material for reflection. On the one hand, the empty tomb calls for a radical faith response, to believe in something strictly on the word of another when we have not witnessed it ourselves. It is also a promise that the tombs of all believers are to ultimately be empty, for death is not an end in itself. Rather, *death itself is empty*, existing purely as the result of Satan's attempts to separate us from God. But the children of God are not to remain in death, not to linger in the grave. They will be joined to God forever through the death and resurrection of Jesus Christ, whose own empty tomb sets the standard for ours.

The prophet Ezekiel relayed the following promise from God: "O my people, I will open your graves and have you rise from them, and bring you back to the land of Israel. Then you shall know that I am the Lord, when I open your graves and have you rise from them, O my people! I will put my spirit in you that you may live, and I will settle you upon your land; thus you shall know that I am the Lord. I have promised, and I will do it, says the Lord" (Ezekiel 37:12-14). This promise was ultimately fulfilled at Easter, and it is in this promise that we hope and rejoice.

As Jesus was preparing to face his own death, he tried to prepare his apostles in these bittersweet verses from the Gospel of John:

"Little children, I'll be with you yet a little while; you'll seek me, and just as I told the Jews, 'Where I'm going you cannot come,' I now tell you also. I give you a new commandment — love one another; as I have loved you, you too should love one another. All will know by this that you're my disciples, if you have love for one another." Simon Peter said to him, "Lord, where are you going?" Jesus answered, "Where I'm going you cannot follow me now, but you'll follow later." (John 13:33-36)

I won't leave you orphaned — I'll come to you. In a little while the world will no longer see me, but you'll see me; because I will live, you, too, will live. On that day you'll realize that I am in my Father, and you in me and I in you. (John 14:18-20)

After Jesus' resurrection, when the news reached the apostles of what had transpired, Thomas refused to believe it until he could put his fingers into Jesus' wounds. Jesus appears before Thomas and offers the chance to do just that. Seeing, Thomas believes. Jesus says that those who believe without seeing are blessed. In a sense, Jesus is also saying to Thomas, "Why do you want to examine the wounds of the past, when I have come to bring you new life?" We all have wounds from our past that we like to dwell upon and keep examining. The risen Jesus asks us, "Why?" Easter has wiped away all the old wounds and has pointed us in a new direction. Through his resurrection Jesus tells us to put the past behind us and walk into a glorious future with him, where the old wounds no longer matter.

Eugene Kennedy writes the following Thanksgiving reflection in his book, *The Pain of Being Human*. I conclude this chapter with its wisdom:

> The good things for which we thank God are stacked like the autumn harvest in our hearts. If we are grateful for all that is good, we may also thank God for things that seem bad. At this last rise before winter, as we brace ourselves against the cold and dark no one can predict, we may thank God that we can feel pain and know sadness, for these are the human sentiments that constitute our glory as well as our grief.
>
> Were we to purge these from our lives, as some try to through a variety of escapes, we would also lose the experiences from which our joy and happiness flow. We would never feel loss in our relationships unless we first knew love. So, too, the terrible feeling of missing someone is the resonation within us of having first succeeded in being close to another human being. Blessed are they who can cry, for their tears attest to their having lived deeply enough to know the meaning of separation and sorrow. For tears shed from love, we thank the Lord.
>
> We are grateful, too, that we bear these scars that are the proof that we have said yes to life, that we are, in the words of psychiatrist Harry Stack Sullivan, much more simply human than anything else. And for that gift of God, in which joy outweighs all pain, we are grateful at Thanksgiving and on every day of the year.

CHAPTER NINE

They Don't Need Another Hero

I have long been a fan of the television series *Leave It To Beaver*. I have seen every episode of that show more times than I care to admit. I find this program not only entertaining, but often enlightening and filled with spiritual wisdom. One of my favorite episodes comes to mind as I conclude this book on fatherhood.

In this show Beaver has an assignment to write a composition on the most interesting character he has ever known. Judy, the class know-it-all, declares that she will write her essay about her father, whom she builds up to be quite a big shot. Beaver decides to write about his father as well, and takes on the challenge of making him seem fascinating to Judy and the rest of his classmates. After following his father around for a day to discover what's interesting about him, Beaver writes the following draft:

> The most interesting character I have ever known is
> my father, Mr. Ward Cleaver. My father was born

right here in this town and still lives in it. He has a very interesting job. He goes to the office every day, except Saturday and Sunday and Christmas and Thanksgiving and all the other holidays and he is also married to my mother and has two sons, me and Wally. The interesting thing he did today was put up screens. He also took the car to get a new fan belt, which was loose. He can fix things and can take a pill without water.

Beaver shows this initial draft to his older brother Wally, who promptly tells him that it's terrible. Instead of making their father seem interesting, it made him sound terribly dull. Beaver asks Wally for help. Deciding to add a little pizzazz, Wally comes up with this version:

The most interesting character I ever knew was my father, Mr. Ward Cleaver. He was born at the mouth of the Amazon, which is a river, and when he was a baby, he was stolen out of his crib by a crocodile, and in the nick of time, he was saved by a friendly head-hunter with a blow gun. During the war, he was a secret general, where he had many interesting experiences. Now he has a job in an office, but he really works for the FBI. On Sundays, he goes to the beach and saves a lot of people from drowning.

While initially finding this version fascinating, Beaver realizes this is not right, either. Telling the truth made his father seem uninteresting; fabricating a story sounded ridiculous. Frustrated that neither the truth nor fiction is making much of an essay, he seeks counsel from his mother. She advises him that instead of writing a list of things his father does, he should write how he *feels* about him, and what his father means to him. Taking this advice to heart, Beaver comes up with his final draft:

> The most interesting character I have ever known is my father, Mr. Ward Cleaver. He does not have an interesting job, he just works hard and takes care of all of us. He never shot things in Africa or saved anybody that was drowning, but that's all right with me because when I am sick he brings me ice cream and when I tell him things or ask him things he always listens to me. He used a whole Saturday to make things in the garage. He may not seem interesting to you or someone because he's not your father, he's mine.

Recently while assisting at a retreat day for second graders in our parish preparing for First Communion, a modern day Judy handed me a jar of paint with an impossibly stuck lid, asking me to open it. As I strained with all my might to no avail she said, "If my dad was here he could do it." "I'd like to see him try!" was what I thought as my muscles quivered, failing to get that jar open! Children throughout the ages have loved to play the "My father can beat your father" game. When dealing with their peers kids want it to seem like their dad is the strongest, fastest, coolest dad there is. Yet it is not extraordinary feats of strength or actions which are heroic in the eyes of the world which truly gain our children's love and admiration. Simply being there for them is the most important thing in the world. Our kids don't need heroes; they need dads. Fatherhood is mainly accomplished in the most mundane, ordinary ways.

In Chapter One I shared a reflection by Kathleen O. Chesto based on the final judgment scene in the Gospel of Matthew. Here I would like to present the actual gospel passage, for it gives us something to think about as fathers:

> When the Son of Man comes in his glory, and all his angels with him, he'll sit on the throne of his glory, and all the nations will be gathered before him, and he'll separate them from each other, the way a shepherd separates the sheep from the goats, and he'll set the sheep at his right hand and the goats at his left hand. Then the King will say to those at his right hand, "Come, you blessed by my Father, receive the kingdom prepared for you from the foundation of the world, for I was hungry and you gave me to eat, I was thirsty and you gave me to drink, I was a stranger and you took me in, naked and you clothed me, I was sick and you cared for me, I was in prison and you came to me." Then the righteous will answer him by saying, "Lord, when did we see you hungry and feed you, or thirsty and give you to drink? When did we see you a stranger and take you in, or naked and clothe you? When did we see you sick, or in prison and come to you?" And in answer the King will say to them, "Amen, I say to you, insofar as you did it for one of these least of my brothers, you did it for me."
>
> (Matthew 25:31-40)

While it is ultimately our faith that gets us into Heaven, faith that is not manifested in good works is useless (see James 2:14-17). Jesus defines the criteria for a genuine faith as the behavior we show to "the least of my brothers." Who is more "least" in the world than children? Our Lord continues to reinforce that he is present most profoundly in children, and that we find our way to him by becoming like children and caring for them.

A fascinating aspect of this passage is that when Jesus tells these people that they served him, they ask, "When did we do this?" At the time they did not see themselves as performing heroic acts worthy of entrance into the heavenly kingdom; they were just doing what they knew in their hearts was the right thing to do. In the eyes of the world their accomplishments were simple; in the eyes of God, they were extraordinary. This reality has two very powerful implications for Christians in general and fathers in particular. The first is what I mentioned above: our most heroic actions are those we don't even recognize as such. Our most effective work as dads may never be made known to us, or it may not be clear until years from now. But even the smallest thing we do for our children will impact them in a great way. We can't become discouraged when our actions may seem minimal to us. No act of love is too small to make an impact on our kids.

Second, as Christians it is important to realize that there are many ways to serve Christ and to find him. Jesus tells us in the Gospel of John that he is the way, the truth, and the life, and that as such he is the only way to the Father (John 14:6). This often causes some Christians to be concerned about people who follow non-Christian religions, or no religion at all. If Jesus is the only way to heaven, then how can those who do not explicitly follow him as Christians get in? This may be a worry for you someday about your own children who may, for whatever reason, stray from the practice of their faith as they get older. But notice that in being welcomed into Heaven, those people expressed puzzlement because they don't even remember serving Jesus. "When did we see you?" Jesus in effect tells them that even though they did not intellectually recognize him, they knew him in their hearts, for their hearts led them to do what Jesus would have commanded them had they heard his word with their ears. Remember that in saying that he is the only way to the Father, Jesus defines who he is: not just the historical figure who lived two thousand years ago and whose life is recorded in the gospels, but *the way, the truth and the life*. It is possible to know the way, the truth and the life without ever having heard the name of Jesus, for God placed an intuitive knowledge of himself in everyone, and he is accessible to everyone who sincerely seeks truth. Thus there are many ways to come to know and serve Jesus — like the people in Matthew's final judgment scene — without consciously recognizing him. Children with a solid foundation in goodness will always walk with Jesus, in one way or another.

Heroes often come in unexpected forms. Jesus commonly called people who did not seem like heroes at all, or who even seemed ill-equipped for the work he was calling them to do. Think about the men he chose to be his apostles. Jesus certainly had a heroic mission to accomplish, and he had his choice of the best and brightest of his day. He gave them two main tasks: to teach people about God, and to heal (Matthew 10:7-8). There were Scripture scholars and leaders of the Temple whom Jesus could have chosen to do the teaching, men who were well educated in the Hebrew Scriptures and the ways of God and articulate teachers and speakers. He did not choose them. There were physicians he could have called upon for his mission of healing. He did not choose them. Instead he chose mainly *fishermen*, who seemingly had no qualifications or experience at all for the kind of work Jesus was looking to do.

What was it about fishermen that made them perfect candidates to become apostles? My limited experience with fishing gives me some possible answers. I fished somewhat as a child. I enjoyed catching them; I dreaded what I had to do from that point on. The excitement of reeling one in was quickly replaced by an aversion to having to handle this creature. I had to hold that cold, scaly, wriggling creature in my hand while I tried to remove the hook. Sometimes the hook was stuck in the lip and easily removed. Other times it was embedded deep inside the fish, and I would have to look inside its disgusting interior to find it. When a hook was really stuck, the fish would squirm and wiggle, making the task of removing the hook even more difficult. The only thing to do in that instance was to hold the fish more firmly and try all the harder to remove the hook.

Perhaps this is what Jesus was thinking of when he called fishermen to do his work. The very reason we need Jesus in the first place is that we're all hooked on sin, and we cannot remove the hook by ourselves. Only Jesus can free us from that hook, and to do it he needs fishermen to help him. Fishermen are not afraid to look deep inside another being, to look at the parts which are not very pretty where hooks are often embedded, in order to help remove them. Fishermen are not afraid to hold someone steady when they would rather squirm away. Fishermen are patient enough to work on the most difficult hooks. Apparently, these were the qualities Jesus was looking for.

Jesus chose people who seemed to be the least qualified to do his important work. In doing so they were not heroes in the eyes of the world, but they were in the eyes of God. We may not believe ourselves qualified or heroic for the vocation of fatherhood, but we are; otherwise God would not have chosen us. We all need to reflect upon what our gifts are, especially those which seem to be the least use to us as fathers, for in those gifts we will most likely find our greatest strengths.

If you need more examples from Scripture or tradition that God's idea of a hero is quite different from the world's, I have some more for you. Consider these words from St. Paul:

> Consider the fact that you were called. Not many of you were wise according to the flesh, nor powerful or well-born, but God chose the foolish things of the world to shame those who are wise, the weak of the world to shame the strong; God chose the base-born and contemptible of the world, things that are nothing, to shame what is, so that the flesh would have nothing to boast of before God. Through God you are in Christ Jesus, and through God Christ became our wisdom, righteousness, sanctification, and redemption, so that as it is written, whoever boasts, let him boast in the Lord.   (1 Corinthians 1:26-31)

When wealthy people are giving large sums of money to the Temple collection, it is a poor widow giving a small amount whom Jesus lauds as a hero (Luke 21:1-4). A woman considered by many to be a notorious sinner is the first one Jesus appears to after his resurrection (John 20:1-16). A convicted criminal in the midst of his shameful execution admits his guilt, recognizes Jesus' goodness, and asks Jesus to remember him; Jesus promises him heaven on the spot (Luke 23:41-43). Joseph of Arimathea and Nicodemus, two followers of Jesus who were afraid to show their allegiance in public, took his body from the cross and gave it a dignified, proper burial (John 19:38-39). St. Thérèse of Lisieux, the Little Flower, was canonized because she found ways to serve God in the very ordinary circumstances of life, not the dramatic. The *Saint Joseph Sunday Missal*, in introducing the readings for the feast of St. Joseph on March 19, states:

> In order to have one's name on the "Who's Who" list, or to be mentioned in the obituary of the national magazines, one must have accomplished something substantial by worldly standards. One must be at least a kind of hero, or in the negative a very controversial figure, if one wants to be remembered in an encyclopedia. St. Joseph, the husband of Mary, would never have qualified.... God's standard of greatness is different from ours.

Darrel Radford shares a beautiful experience of finding the unexpected heroics of fatherhood in a chapter of *Chicken Soup for the Baseball Fan's Soul*. A devoted Cincinnati Reds fan, Mr. Radford brought his five-year-old daughter Molly to her first Reds game, excited to introduce his little girl to the hallowed tradition of Cincinnati baseball. He would explain the game to her, tell her all about the "Big Red Machine" championship teams he grew up rooting for, initiate her into "the wave," the seventh inning stretch and other traditions. He had it all planned. What he did not plan on was the rain which began pouring down as they arrived after their two-hour drive to the stadium. As the ground crew began to put the tarp on the field his spirits sank as he saw this dream he had long anticipated — being a dad and bringing his child to a baseball game — melt in the rain.

Much to his surprise, Molly found beauties in the ballpark he had seen many times but had never appreciated. She was actually fascinated by the intricate choreography of the ground crew as they worked together to place the tarp on the field. While the highlight film of the Reds' past glory played on the stadium scoreboard screen, Molly introduced her dad to the pleasures of running up and down stadium ramps screaming at the top of one's lungs. In an experience where he saw only disappointment, Molly had found joy. Mr. Radford learned that day to "become like little children," and realized that the heroism of fatherhood comes not in exposing your child to dramatic experiences, but simply being with them and sharing in the wonder of their lives:

> Fatherhood is grand, no matter what the weather. If you pay attention and are receptive to your children, it's an event that never gets postponed. Just when things are bad, there is a ramp right around the corner leading to a shining moment. World Series heroes are nothing compared to the magic found within your own children. All you have to do is just look.
>
> I'll never forget that day with Molly. The day we

went to my favorite ballpark and never sat in our seats. The day we went to see the Reds and watched the ground crew instead. The day I didn't see a single inning of baseball but came away from the stadium more exhilarated than ever. Not because the Reds won, but because I was a dad.

Enjoy playing God. It's the greatest thing you'll ever do.

Works Cited

Scripture texts from the Old Testament are from *The New American Bible,* copyright © 1970 by the Confraternity of Christian Doctrine. New Testament texts are from *The New Testament: St. Paul Catholic Edition,* copyright © 2000 by the Society of St. Paul.

Albom, Mitch. *Tuesdays With Morrie.* (New York: Doubleday, 1997).

"Blessed Luigi Beltrame Quattrocchi." *Savior.org.*

Burney, Joan & Chandler, Phyllis. *Sharing the Faith With Your Child.* (Liguori, MO: Liguori, 1984).

Catechism of the Catholic Church. (Washington, DC: United States Catholic Conference, 1994).

"Cat's in the Cradle" is from *Verities & Balderdash* by Harry Chapin, copyright © 1974, Elektra Records.

Champlin, Joseph M. "10 Questions About Annulment." *Catholic Update,* October, 2002.

Chaput, Charles J. *Living the Catholic Faith: Rediscovering the Basics.* (Ann Arbor, MI: Charis, 2001).

Chesto, Kathleen O. *Family Centered Intergenerational Religious Education.* (New York: Sheed & Ward, 1988).

Coffey, Kathy. *Experiencing God With Your Children.* (New York: Crossroad, 1997).

Dickens, Charles. *A Christmas Carol.* (New York: Doubleday, 1991).

Finley, Mitch. *For Men Only: Strategies for Living Catholic.* (Liguori, MO: Liguori, 1998).

Hahn, Scott. *The Lamb's Supper: The Mass as Heaven on Earth.* (New York: Doubleday, 1999).

Kennedy, Eugene. *The Pain of Being Human.* (New York: Crossroad, 1997).

The Liturgy of the Hours. (New York: Catholic Book Publishing Company, 1975).

Lumen Gentium. (Collegeville, MN: The Liturgical Press, 1992).

McGrath, Tom. *Raising Faith-Filled Kids.* (Chicago: Loyola, 2000).

Mother Teresa. *A Simple Path.* (New York: Ballantine, 1995).

New Saint Joseph Sunday Missal. (New York: Catholic Book Publishing Company, 1986).

Our Hearts Were Burning Within Us. (Washington, DC: United States Catholic Conference, 1999).

Payesko, Robert. *The Truth About Mary*, Vol. 2. (Santa Barbara, CA: Queenship Pub., 1997).

Pope John Paul II. *Evangelium Vitae*, 1995.
    Familiaris Consortio, 1981.
    Homily of October 21, 2001.
    Letter to Families, 1994.
    Letter to Women, 1995.
    Mulieris Dignitatum, 1988.

Radford, Darrel. "The Best Game I Never Saw." *Chicken Soup For the Baseball Fan's Soul.* (Deerfield Beach, FL: Health Communications, Inc., 2001).

Rites of the Catholic Church. (Collegeville, MN: The Liturgical Press, 1990).

Sullivan, Mary Ann. "Heroic in Marriage." *Marian Helper*, Spring, 2002.

ST PAULS

This book was produced by St. Pauls/Alba House, the Society of St. Paul, an international religious congregation of priests and brothers dedicated to serving the Church through the communications media.

For information regarding this and associated ministries of the Pauline Family of Congregations, write to the Vocation Director, Society of St. Paul, P.O. Box 189, 9531 Akron-Canfield Road, Canfield, Ohio 44406-0189. Phone (330) 702-0359; or E-mail: spvocationoffice@aol.com or check our internet site, www.albahouse.org